A Year in the Life of the Universe

A Seasonal Guide
to Viewing the Cosmos

Text by Robert Gendler
Foreword by Timothy Ferris

Voyageur Press

First published in 2006 by Voyageur Press, an imprint of MBI Publishing Company,
Galtier Plaza, Suite 200, 380 Jackson Street, St. Paul, MN 55101-3885 USA

Additional Photograph Credits

Photographs © Jim Misti/Robert Gendler: pp. 11, 32, 39, 42, 43 (bottom), 47, 48, 73, 75 (bottom), 76, 79, 82, 90, 92 (top right), 99, 100, 102, 103, 105, 108, 109, 110, 111, 112, 113, 115, 119, 121, 123, 127, 134, 135 (top), 137, 138, 139, 140, and 141.

Photographs © Volker Wendel/Bernd Flach-Wilken: pp. 21, 29, 33, 49, 77, 120, and 142.

Photographs © Stan Moore: pp. 23 and 133.

Photographs © Daniel Verschatse: pp. 30, 35, 114, and 118.

Photographs © Russell Croman: pp. 34 and 151.

Photographs © Josch Hambsch/Robert Gendler: pp. 37 and 58.

Photograph © Hubble Space Telescope: p. 38 (top).

Photographs © Brad Moore: pp. 64 and 91.

Photographs © Eddie Trimarchi: pp. 94 and 129.

Photograph © Daniel Verschatse/Volker Wendel/Bernd Flach-Wilken/Robert Gendler: p. 117.

Photographs © Wei-Hao Wang: pp. 124 and 128.

Photograph © Martin Pugh/Robert Gendler: p. 130.

Photograph © Allan Cook/Adam Block/NOAO/AURA/NSF: p. 132.

MBI Publishing Company titles are also available at discounts in bulk quantity for industrial or sales-promotional use. For details write
to Special Sales Manager at MBI Publishing Company, Galtier Plaza, Suite 200, 380 Jackson Street, St. Paul, MN 55101-3885 USA

All-sky star charts compliments of *Sky & Telescope* magazine © 2006 New Track Media LLC.

Library of Congress Cataloging-in-Publication Data

Gendler, Robert.
  A year in the life of the universe : a seasonal guide to viewing the cosmos / Robert Gendler ; with a foreword by Timothy Ferris.
    p. cm.
  ISBN-13: 978-0-7603-2642-8
  ISBN-10: 0-7603-2642-8
  1. Astronomy–Observers' manuals. 2. Galaxies–Observers' manuals. 3. Nebulae–Observers' manuals. 4. Astronomy–Pictorial works. I. Title.
  QB64.G427 2006
  520.22'3–dc22

                                    2006003503

Edited by Danielle J. Ibister
Designed by Jennifer Bergstrom

Printed in China

On the frontispiece: Andromeda Galaxy.
On the title pages, large photo: Rosette Nebula.
On the title pages, small photo: M66.

This book is dedicated to my wife, Joanne; to my children, James and Gianna; and to the memory of my sister Susan.

Acknowledgments

I'd like to acknowledge several institutions and individuals who were critical to the successful completion of this book. Without question my first debt of gratitude goes to my publisher, Voyageur Press. In particular, I am grateful to Michael Dregni, who saw the book's potential and nurtured the project from the beginning, and to Danielle Ibister, who edited the text and whose guidance was indispensable toward developing the final draft. In the same context and with no less enthusiasm, I'd like to thank Sky Publishing for its editorial partnership in the project and specifically Valerie Coffey, who edited the scientific content of the book. In particular, I am grateful to Marcy McCreary, who did much of the initial groundwork and orchestrated the early process of getting the project up and running. I owe much thanks to Rick Fienberg, the editor in chief at *Sky & Telescope* magazine, who showed unwavering support and enthusiasm for the project from the beginning and who provided a steady supply of thoughtful advice and help when obstacles arose. I also want to thank Paul Deans at Sky Publishing for his help and editorial assistance.

I am particularly grateful to Jim Misti, who contributed greatly to the quality of the book by providing data for a substantial subset of images which I later processed. Jim was kind enough to offer high-quality image data for selected images, which he took with his 32-inch telescope (or, as Jim likes to call it, his "big eye in the sky") from his observatory in the Arizona desert. Jim's generous support went beyond providing image data and included some helpful editorial suggestions and, not the least, his friendship and unwavering support for the project, of which I am most appreciative. I'd like to thank Josch Hambsch, Daniel Verschatse, Russell Croman, Volker Wendel, Bernd Flach-Wilken, Adam Block, Johannes Schedler, Stan Moore, Eddie Trimarchi, Wei-Hao Wang, and Brad Moore for allowing me to use some of their fine images to round out the selection of southern and other objects I was unable to capture. This acknowledgement would of course be incomplete without expressing utmost gratitude to my wife, Joanne, and to my children, James and Gianna, for putting up with the rigorous commitment in time and energy that this avocation and book required.

Horsehead Nebula

CONTENTS

IC 1805

Spring The Realm of the Galaxies   87

Summer The Milky Way: Coming Home   125

FOREWORD

———————————●———————————

Stargazers have been creating images of the wonders revealed by their telescopes ever since the telescope was invented. Galileo, the first scientist to train a telescope on the night sky, immediately started making drawings to record his observations of planets and stars. He did a pretty good job of it, too: His drawings showing the positions of Jupiter's satellites, for instance, when matched against computer re-creations of their actual locations in the sky, prove to be as precisely accurate as the sharpness of his pencils would permit. Galileo's high standard was equaled or exceeded by Christiaan Huygens's sketches of Saturn in the late 1600s, Johann Schröter's 1791–1802 atlas of the moon, and Giovanni Schiaparelli's nineteenth-century renderings of Mars, all of which are both scientifically useful and often sufficiently evocative to approach the status of art.

Photography was applied to astronomy from its very inception; indeed it was an astronomer, John Herschel, who coined the word "photography." John William Draper, who in 1839 took the first photograph of a human face, also made the first photograph of the moon the following year. Edward Emerson Barnard, who grew up poor in Nashville during the Civil War and was put to work in a photographer's gallery at age eight, taught himself astronomy and turned his old portrait lens on the sky to reveal the intricate glowing gas and dust clouds of the Milky Way. Color astrophotography flourished in the hands of darkroom wizards such as William C. Miller, whose 1958 color image of the Andromeda Galaxy, taken through the 48-inch Schmidt camera at Palomar a half century ago, has been reprinted millions of times and still shows up on college dorm-room walls today.

A print of Miller's memorable Andromeda photo hangs in my observatory as well— next to a larger, more detailed, and even more aesthetically impressive photograph of the same galaxy. This superior photo was made not by a professional astronomer using a mountaintop telescope costing millions of dollars but by the amateur astronomer Robert Gendler, using a small telescope that he rolled out each night onto the driveway in front of his home in suburban Connecticut. (Rob's equipment in those days included a black cloth on a long pole that he would drape over a nearby streetlight to cut off its glare.) It is one of many heavenly portraits that have brought Rob recognition as one of the most accomplished astrophotographers in the world.

A trio of technological advances made his attainments possible. First, high-quality telescopes became more affordable and easier to use than ever before. Second, the CCD ("charge-coupled device") imaging chip, which was invented at Bell Labs in 1969 and originally was fragile, balky, and dauntingly expensive, evolved into a cheaper and more light-sensitive alternative to photographic film. Third, the advent of personal computers enabled amateur astronomers to readily operate CCD cameras, process the images they produced, and disseminate them over the Internet.

Technology in itself cannot, however, produce art. What a new technology can do—from the spread of Dutch and Italian oil paints in the seventeenth century to digital microprocessors today—is put tools with artistic potential in the hands of many people, some of whom use them in surprisingly original ways. Rob Gendler is one of the most talented of these innovators. Inspired by the astronomical photographs he saw on display in the Hayden Planetarium in New York when he was a boy, Rob began thinking about trying his hand at astrophotography once he had completed his medical training and moved to Connecticut, where the stars beckoned from darker skies. He spent a year learning the constellations before purchasing a simple telescope for visual observing. Later, he moved up to a computerized telescope and digital camera.

"I felt compelled," he recalls, "by the sense of discovery that truly ancient photons traveling over millions of years could be recorded in a matter of minutes." Initially, Rob would photograph dozens of galaxies, nebulae, and star clusters in a single night, but as he improved his craftsmanship, he sometimes spent several entire nights recording the light from a single object in order to bring out its subtle details. When he had virtually exhausted the Connecticut skies—which though darker than Manhattan's are still far from ideal—Rob had a 20-inch telescope installed at an inky-dark, high-altitude site in New Mexico. He operates this new telescope remotely, over the Internet. "It's a blast to be able to do this," he told me. "For years I dealt with frozen finger tips in the Connecticut winters and the growing problem of suburban light pollution. Now I could image under dark skies and do it all from the comfort of my home."

Rob's boyhood memories of the photos he saw at the Hayden Planetarium remain vivid. "All my images today are attempts to actualize those visions burned into my impressionable mind many years ago," he recently wrote. "They are what inspired me then and what still inspires me now. Their staggering detail and penetrating depth, spread over a large panoramic field, is what I try to emulate when I plan my big projects. I may not succeed in accomplishing this but I try."

In truth, Rob not only tries to equal the efforts of the top modern professionals but often surpasses them. When the Hubble Space Telescope team released an image that they described as the largest mosaic of a nearby galaxy ever made, they had to correct their press release the next day: Rob, they were reminded, had recently made an even larger mosaic, of the Andromeda Galaxy. He has pioneered several other innovative techniques such as using image data taken by different instruments to achieve unique compositions while optimizing detail. He favors what he calls "the childlike attitude of experimentation and exploration, the willingness to deviate from the dogma of traditional imaging."

Art has been defined as "reality filtered through a sensibility." The reality in Rob's imagery stretches far and wide in space and time, ranging from the baroque beauty of our own Milky Way to that of other galaxies millions of light years away, each in some sense incomprehensible yet each utterly and inescapably real, looming in the sky with the calm persistence of an unanswered question. The sensibility through which Rob filters this vast reality is admirably modest and respectful of the facts—this is how these star clusters, nebulae, and galaxies really look, or would look were our eyes better at seeing in the dark—yet has an aesthetic flare all its own. Rob's work evinces the affable good taste of a top professional guide, who presents you with breathtaking natural spectacles and stays out of the way, so that only later on, reflecting on the experience, do you realize how much you owe that guide. Enjoy the view; then go out and have a look for yourself.

Timothy Ferris
Rocky Hill Observatory

Orion Nebulosity

PREFACE

My infatuation with the universe began as a child in the theater of the Hayden Planetarium in New York City. It was there under the planetarium dome that I first became captivated by space, planets, galaxies, and the vast unseen universe. The planetarium's daytime show electrified my imagination with unthinkable scales of distance and time. Its impact had a durable effect that carried through to my adult life.

In that era, astrophotography consisted of black-and-white film images of magnificent spiral galaxies and great nebulae taken by large professional observatories. I didn't realize it at the time, but those memorable images of distant worlds in the blackness of space would become the seeds of a serious future avocation.

Later on in my adult life when I became serious about astrophotography, my guiding light of astronomical information was Hans Vehrenberg's *Atlas of Deep-Sky Splendors*. In its time, the book was a superb resource of beautiful astrophotographs coupled with thoughtful and informative text. The pages of an important book show the wear and tear of frequent forays into its rich chapters. My atlas had the look of a book that was used often and used well, as it satisfied my hunger for information and guidance. Even in later years, when its contents inevitably became outdated, I found myself returning to it for inspiration as the author's love for his subject was evident in every word and photograph.

As time went on, there was no shortage of good astronomy books; however, nothing else carried the torch of Vehrenberg's fine atlas. A void existed in the amateur astronomy world that was longing to be filled. I sensed a need for a general astronomy book showcasing the sky's most spectacular jewels in an organized, coherent way that would appeal to the less experienced reader. This book was conceived with that goal in mind.

I chose to present the objects in order according to their right ascension, beginning at the autumnal equinox and progressing through the four seasons. In this way, the objects are presented as they appear throughout a solar year, making for easy and simple identification and referencing. (The seasons are, of course, reversed in the southern hemisphere, and for the sake of simplicity, the southern objects have been incorporated into northern seasons.)

Due to size restrictions, I was forced to limit the book to a relatively small subset from many thousands of objects that, in my opinion, stood out by virtue of their beauty, visual impact, and scientific interest. I am aware of the subjective nature involved in choosing and excluding objects according to personal preference and apologize in advance for the necessity to do so.

My hope is that the basic structure of the book as an atlas of quality images arranged by season and accompanied by meaningful text will find a useful niche among astronomy books available today. Aside from the beautiful images, the more advanced reader will find current and meaningful descriptive data. For the novice astronomer, the book will be a helpful resource to get started and to return to, as he or she grows in knowledge and experience. For those who have only a casual interest in astronomy but who have a desire for excellent astrophotography from an artistic or nature perspective, the book's first-rate images should satisfy that craving.

INTRODUCTION

Since antiquity, humans have craved knowledge of what lies beyond our small, isolated world. Only recently have we begun to understand the physical processes driving the cosmological world. This understanding has not come easily. Brilliant and curious minds have toiled over centuries to assemble the knowledge we enjoy today. The cosmos continues to yield its secrets reluctantly and slowly. The forces of physics and chemistry have shaped a universe that not only embodies beauty of the highest order but is also strange and mysterious beyond anything the imagination can summon.

The night sky is mostly invisible to the unaided human eye, except for the moon, planets, and bright stars. Fortunately, a modest telescope can reveal thousands of distant worlds beyond our own solar system, even beyond our galaxy. However, we soon become aware of a very real limitation. Due to enormous distance and exceedingly low levels of light, the objects we see through the telescope are without color or detailed form. Sooner or later, our senses long for a more intense visual experience. It is no surprise that we have used photography to satisfy that longing.

Astrophotography was born a few years after Louis Daguerre created his first daguerreotype in 1839. Photographs were soon being made of the sun, moon, and planets. In 1880, the first photograph was made of a nebula—a cloud of dust and gas illuminated by starlight. Astrophotography quickly evolved into a useful technological tool for gathering astronomical data. In 1923, Edwin Hubble photographed and later recognized extragalactic stars in what had formerly been called the Andromeda "nebula." His photographs revealed an island universe similar in many respects to our Milky Way. Until that time, astronomers believed the Milky Way to be the only galaxy in the universe. With the discovery of the Andromeda Galaxy came the realization that ours is one of countless galaxies. Our perspective and place in the cosmos was dramatically and immutably changed.

M95

Astrophotography evolved rapidly over the last century. Film has given way to the digital world of the charge-coupled device (CCD) camera and computer. We are now witnessing an enormous revolution in knowledge as a deluge of information is brought to us through the science of electronic imaging. Modern astroimaging has brought the distant universe closer and in extraordinary detail and brilliant color.

Aside from scientific understanding, the celestial world has proved itself worthy of artistic representation and expression. It is toward these ends, the scientific and the artistic, that I hope this book and its images will reach people and evoke admiration and a deeper understanding for nature on a grand scale. Enjoy the journey!

SHORT COURSE ON ASTRONOMY

The following abbreviated treatment of broad astronomical principles and concepts is not by any means intended to substitute for a formal course in astronomy. Its purpose is to simply provide the uninitiated reader a resource for understanding the nature of the objects presented in the pages ahead.

Astronomical Distances

Fundamental to understanding the universe is grasping the vast scales of distance and size beyond the boundaries of our own small world. The transformation of the two-dimensional sky to the three dimensions we know today is a great tribute to human ingenuity. Distances to deep-sky objects (objects beyond our solar system) are measured in light years. A light year is the distance light travels in one year, or about 6 trillion miles, or 63,241 times the distance between the earth and sun. Knowing that light can circle the earth seven times in one second is humbling and gives a basic grasp of the immense scales of distance to even "nearby" deep-sky objects in our own galaxy.

Many of the stars we see in the night sky are within 100 light years of earth. The closest star to earth is Alpha Centauri at about 4 light years. Common nebulae and star clusters in our galaxy reside several hundred to several thousand light years away. The Milky Way, our parent galaxy, stretches 100,000 light years across and contains some 200 billion stars. Traveling at conventional spacecraft speeds, traversing the galaxy would require over one billion years!

The next step up in distance is the intergalactic scale. The closest galaxy similar to our own is the Andromeda Galaxy at a distance of 2.5 million light years. When we look at Andromeda, we see light that began its journey toward Earth at the dawn of human evolution. When those ancient photons are received by our retinas or cameras, we have an opportunity to gaze back in time as if looking through a cosmic time machine. As another example, the Virgo cluster of galaxies released the light we see today at an epoch coinciding with the extinction of the dinosaurs and the rise of the mammals and primates, our ancient ancestors.

The Life and Death of Stars

Most processes occurring in the visible universe involve stars in some way. In fact, all elements, with just a few exceptions, were formed in the nuclear furnaces of stars. This includes the heavier elements such as carbon and oxygen, the main constituents of living organisms. The exceptions are hydrogen, deuterium, helium, and lithium, which were created in the big bang.

Astronomers classify stars using many schemes, including brightness, color, temperature, size, mass, and association with other stars. The Greek astronomer Hipparchus first characterized stars by brightness in the second century AD. His system of magnitude is still in use today. Hipparchus divided stars by visual brightness from magnitude 1 (brightest) to magnitude 6 (faintest). Each level represents a 2.5-fold change in brightness. With the arrival of the telescope and later the camera, stars as faint as magnitude 30 became detectable (four billion times fainter than could be observed with the naked eye).

Perhaps most helpful to understanding the true nature of stars is description by color and surface temperature. A star is powered by hydrogen fusion deep in its core, where temperatures typically reach 15 million degrees Kelvin. (The Kelvin scale is based on the temperature in an absolute vacuum of 0 degrees Kelvin, which equals -273 degrees Celsius or -459 degrees Fahrenheit.) The fusion of hydrogen to helium releases prodigious amounts of energy in this core. The energy travels slowly to the star's surface before it is released in diverse forms, including heat, light, and radiation. The surface temperature of a star produces the star's color in the same way any radiative body has a color depending on its temperature. The amount of energy released at the surface is in turn related to the temperature and mass of the star's core.

The modern and most meaningful way of characterizing and analyzing stars is by spectral class. Today, we classify stars by the letters OBAFGKM. (The famous mnemonic for remembering this sequence is Oh, Be A Fine Girl, Kiss Me.) A star's spectral class is defined by its characteristics of temperature, size, and density. The hottest and most massive stars are in the O and B classes and typically emit blue to white light. Stars of intermediate temperature and mass range from A- to G-type and emit white to yellow light. The coolest, least massive stars are K- and M-type and emit orange to red light. Two new classes have been added (L and T) to account for the recent discovery of very low-mass stars.

Our sun is a yellow G-type star with a temperature of 5,780 degrees Kelvin. Surface temperatures of stars typically range from 40,000 degrees Kelvin (O-type) to 3,000 degrees Kelvin (M-type). The mass of stars can range from greater than one hundred times to one-eighth the mass of our sun (defined as 1 solar mass). Thus, the mass of stars can range from 100 to 0.125 solar masses. Below this lower limit, nuclear fusion cannot occur.

Stars vary in composition. Typically, stars are made predominantly of hydrogen. A rare and exotic breed is the Wolf-Rayet star, which is dominated by helium. These extremely hot and luminous stars have surface temperatures exceeding 50,000 degrees Kelvin and can shine with the brightness of over a million suns. First described by the French astronomers Charles Wolf and Georges Rayet in 1867, Wolf-Rayet stars represent a late evolutionary phase of massive O-type blue supergiant stars. Astronomers estimate that only one in ten million stars is a Wolf-Rayet. Fewer than two hundred have been identified in the Milky Way.

Despite their limited numbers, Wolf-Rayets contribute substantially to the ecology of galaxies by infusing the galactic disk with heavier elements such as carbon, oxygen, neon, nitrogen, and magnesium. These elements then become incorporated into subsequent generations of stars and possibly their planet progeny. Heavier elements are essential to the evolution of living organisms, so it is possible that ancient Wolf-Rayets played a role in the establishment of life on Earth.

Stars that are actively fusing hydrogen to helium, such as our sun, are called main-sequence stars. In essence, stars are defined by their ability to generate energy by fusion. Stars generally spend about 90 percent of their lives on the main sequence. When stars exhaust their hydrogen fuel, they begin the inevitable process of stellar death. At this point in their evolution, they begin to leave the main sequence. The lifetime of a star is directly related to its mass. The most massive stars rapidly use up their fuel and may live only a few million years. This is in contrast to lower-mass stars, such as our sun, which may enjoy a main-sequence life of over ten billion years.

When a sunlike star exhausts its hydrogen core and begins to die, a new process begins. Helium fuses to carbon and later to oxygen, which will sustain the star for a short period but at the expense of further core collapse, higher core temperatures, and continued surface expansion. The surface of the star, no longer checked by gravity, bloats and cools. At this stage, it is referred to as a red giant. The bloated diameter can exceed ten times that of our sun. The star begins a futile cycle of further core collapse and surface expansion that can end either passively as a white dwarf surrounded by a "planetary" nebula or, for more massive stars, in a cataclysmic explosion known as a supernova.

Planetary Nebulae

Late in its life, the activity of a low- or intermediate-mass star (0.8 to 10 solar masses) like our sun results in a planetary nebula. As the gravity of the dying star weakens, its outer envelope is expelled into space. The hot shrunken core releases abundant radiation, which catches up to and collides with older gas clouds released earlier. The interaction creates a dazzling display of brilliant colors. The entire complex is called a planetary nebula. They have nothing to do with planets but received their name from eighteenth-century astronomer William Herschel, who likened them to planets because of their shape. The remaining compact core of the star is known as a white dwarf, which can no longer produce energy by nuclear fusion but instead produces copious radiation and heat by virtue of its extremely high density.

Supernovae

High-mass stars (greater than 10 solar masses) have a different evolution. Initially, they follow a similar path as red giants. But because they have considerably higher reserves of mass, they are capable of much higher core temperatures and therefore can fuse heavier elements. Already relatively huge, they become red supergiants as they leave the main sequence. Their outer envelopes can extend almost the diameter of our solar system. Their cores fuse increasingly heavier elements such as neon, magnesium, oxygen, and later, sulfur and silicon. Finally, silicon and sulfur fuse to iron, which cannot undergo further fusion.

In the end, gravity triumphs. The star can no longer support itself. For these furious supergiants, the end comes with a catastrophic collapse of the stellar core followed by an enormous discharge of energy that tears through the remaining envelope and destroys the star. The incredible release of energy is so powerful that, for a few days after the explosion, the light output exceeds that of an entire galaxy. This is known as a supernova. The light output makes them easily visible in distant galaxies. Supernovae are rare events, occurring in a given galaxy maybe two or three times a century. The last one observed from Earth in our own galaxy was in 1604 and it was bright enough to be visible in daylight. Because of their rarity, we learn about supernovae by observing them in other galaxies.

What happens to the core and outer envelope of a very massive star after a supernova blast? If the core is 1.4 to 3 times the mass of the sun, it collapses down to what is called a neutron star. Only about six hundred are known to exist. Neutron stars have incredible density, given that the core of the former star now exists in a space only a few miles wide. The density exceeds 100 million tons per cubic centimeter. Neutron stars tend to spin many times a second, releasing abundant energy in the form of radio waves, X-rays, and gamma rays. Such neutron stars are called pulsars.

If the mass of the stellar core is great enough, collapse continues forever. The result is an enigmatic object called a black hole. Gravity is so strong in a black hole that even light cannot escape. We only surmise the presence of black holes as they cannot be directly observed.

The outer envelope and core material blown into space after a supernova continues to expand in a shell called a supernova remnant. As this material smashes into surrounding gas clouds, it creates shock fronts and releases energy. The clouds can glow in visual wavelengths, revealing brilliant colors and shapes—making them excellent subjects for astrophotographers.

Star Clusters

Stars are not formed one at a time, but in groups called clusters. Once the ancestral cloud disperses, the groupings are called open clusters, with loosely bound stars spaced on average about one light year apart. Open clusters range from as few as ten young stars to as many as three thousand. All the members of an open cluster originate from the same molecular cloud and therefore have several important characteristics in common: They are the same age, the same initial chemical composition, the same distance from Earth, and they move with the same velocity and in the same direction. Our sun was once a member of an open cluster but has long since left its stellar siblings.

Globular clusters are spherical collections of mostly ancient stars numbering between tens of thousands to a million or more stars and stretching 100 to 300 light years across. They are truly ancient structures with a minimum age of about eleven billion years. Most are believed to have formed at the same time as their parent galaxy. The cluster members are mostly highly evolved low-mass main sequence stars.

Nebulae

In the pretelescope era, the word "nebula" was used by observers to describe any fuzzy, or nebulous, patch in the night sky that wasn't sharp like a planet or star. Charles Messier, the eighteenth-century French comet hunter, rejected—but fortunately cataloged—these nebulae as comet "imposters." With the advent of the telescope, camera, and spectroscope, we now know that nebulae are vast clouds of interstellar dust and gas. These clouds are often made visible by interactions with nearby stars.

The "stuff" between stars is known as the interstellar medium. The interstellar medium condenses to form giant molecular clouds, which are the essential places of star birth. The molecular clouds comprise 1 percent dust particles and 99 percent gas. Of the gas, 90 percent is hydrogen and 10 percent helium. As molecular clouds orbit a galaxy, they interact with other clouds, spiral arms of galaxies, and supernovae, all of which trigger fragmentation. Once the cloud begins to fragment, individual "cores" form. Under the influence of gravity, the cores contract further and generate heat. As temperature and density rise, protostars form, which eventually give rise to fledgling stars and star clusters. The new stars, in turn, interact with their ancestral cloud to form various types of nebulae.

Nebulae can be distinguished by the chemical and physical processes that occur within them. Emission nebulae represent bright clouds of fluorescing ionized hydrogen (HII) energized by very hot, young stars. Also known as HII regions, the gas clouds exist in an ionized state. Some stars (massive O- and B-types) pour large amounts of ultraviolet radiation into the interstellar medium. The radiation is absorbed by the hydrogen gas in the clouds and re-released in the form of mostly red light. HII regions are numerous in the arms of spiral galaxies such as our Milky Way.

Reflection nebulae reflect the light of stars embedded in clouds of dust. The clouds consist of microscopic particles of heavier elements such as oxygen, silicon, and carbon. The starlight reflects off the dust particles and scatters in the shorter blue wavelengths. Reflection nebulae, therefore, typically have the characteristic blue color of reflected starlight.

Absorption nebulae, also known as dark nebulae, absorb light. These dark clouds of gas and dust are made visible only by the light of bright stars or bright nebulae behind them. They do not emit or reflect light. Dark nebulae are often found in and adjacent to emission and reflection nebulae and can be places of active star formation.

Special circumstances give rise to special classes of nebulae, such as Wolf-Rayet nebulae. These emission nebulae are the outcome of the enormous energy output and fierce stellar winds of Wolf-Rayet stars. These stars can lose two-thirds of their mass during this final stage of stellar life, creating winds in excess of 3 million miles per hour. The winds can produce enormous windblown bubbles, illuminated by the central blue star.

While planetary nebulae and supernova remnants may last only several thousand years, an emission nebula can exist for a million years or more before its gases disperse from the radiation and stellar winds of its stellar progeny. The larger molecular clouds, the progenitor clouds of stars and star clusters, can exist for tens of millions of years.

The Realm of the Galaxies

If stars form the building blocks of galaxies, then galaxies form the building blocks of our universe. Galaxies are vast rotating systems of stars, gas, and dust. Galactic dimensions can exceed our ability to comprehend the enormous scales of size, distance, and time that define their existence. Galaxies range in size from dwarf types, only a few thousand light years across, to great spiral and elliptical galaxies spanning several hundred thousand light years. They contain anywhere from a few million to as many as one trillion stars.

The true nature of a galaxy was not apparent until Edwin Hubble's epochal discovery of extragalactic stars in Andromeda. He reported his findings in 1929, and the paradigm of the universe was changed forever.

Andromeda is the closest galaxy similar to our own Milky Way. These two are among some forty other galaxies that make up the Local Group of galaxies. Our Local Group, together with several other nearby groups plus the nearby Virgo cluster, make up the Local Supercluster. The supercluster contains many thousands of galaxies. There are probably tens of millions of superclusters in the observable universe.

Like stars and nebulae, galaxies can be classified by a variety of schemes. The simplest and easiest is by form. Galaxy types can be spiral, lenticular, elliptical, and irregular. Spiral galaxies, which make up more than half of all observed galaxies, show the most complex and dynamic structure and the greatest degree of organization. A spiral galaxy has a basic flat shape, similar to a Frisbee but with a central bulge. The spiral arms exist in a relatively thin, flat disk that rotates around the central nucleus. Massive amounts of dust, gas, and stars rotate in the disk and compose the star-forming regions of the galaxy. It is within the huge spiral arms that new stars, star clusters, and nebulae form. Our Milky Way has several distinct spiral arms known as the Perseus, Sagittarius, Orion, and Carina arms, among others. We reside in the Orion arm.

Spirals can have dramatically different appearances depending on their orientation in space and the inclination of the disk to our line of sight. When viewed "edge-on," a spiral galaxy will appear as an elongated structure split by its dark, thin equatorial disk. Viewed "face-on," the spiral pattern becomes clearly visible. There are of course many variations between the two extremes depending on the angle of inclination.

A special class of galaxies are known as active galaxies. These luminous galaxies release copious amounts of energy that cannot be accounted for by stellar processes. All active galaxies have in common an active galactic nucleus (AGN), a compact engine that expels spectacular jets of high-velocity gaseous matter. The conventional belief is that AGNs are the product of supermassive black holes.

What is the origin of a spiral structure? The most popular theory to date, devised by C. C. Lin and Frank Shu in 1964, is that "density waves" propagate through the spiral disk. The stars rotate around the galactic center at about twice the speed as the density wave. (One rotation of the stars in the sun's vicinity takes 230 million years in the Milky Way. Our sun has made twenty trips around the galactic center.) The stars tend to clump together as they encounter the density wave, compressing the interstellar gas and leading to bursts of new star formation. Many questions about galaxy dynamics and evolution remain unanswered, such as what created the density waves in the first place.

Cosmology

Since the dawn of humanity, people have struggled to understand the origin and fate of the universe. The last few centuries have witnessed a greater understanding of the universe with all its peculiarities. Despite a greater understanding, it has become clear that the cosmos may be even more mysterious than we ever imagined. That said, we do know something about how the universe got its start. The big bang theory is currently the accepted explanation of the origin and evolution of the universe as we know it. It forms the backbone of modern cosmology.

The Big Bang theory postulates that the universe came into existence from a small "singularity" in a single instant 13 to 14 billion years ago. Early on, it was hot and dense. It underwent inflation and eventually cooled to reach its current size and temperature, eventually forming the stars and galaxies we observe today. The unprecedented accuracy of recent observations leaves little doubt about the validity of the Big Bang theory. Three key observations laid the groundwork for the theory. The first was Edwin Hubble's observation in 1929 that the galaxies were receding from us in all directions. The second is the existence of the light elements hydrogen, helium, and lithium, which could only have formed from the fusion of protons and neutrons in the first few minutes after the Big Bang. The last is the 1965 discovery of cosmic microwave background radiation, which is believed to be the primordial remnant of heat energy left over from the Big Bang.

Coordinates and Catalogs

An essential tool to understanding and navigating the sky is the celestial sphere. This model divides the sky into a coordinate system, mapping each celestial object on an imaginary sphere in the sky, as if they were all equidistant from Earth. There are north and south celestial poles and a celestial equator. The celestial sphere's reference grid is analogous to longitude and latitude but instead called right ascension and declination, respectively. The right ascension is split into twenty-four parts called sidereal hours and tells us an object's position in the east-west direction. It also provides information as to which time of the year the object is visible. Declination tells us the object's location in the north-south orientation. Each deep-sky object has a fixed set of celestial coordinates.

The other essential element to navigating the sky is the organization of deep-sky objects into various catalogs. Many astronomers have cataloged celestial objects throughout history, but without question the most famous is the Messier catalog of 110 of the brightest and most spectacular deep-sky objects. A comet hunter, Messier cataloged numerous "diffuse glows" that later turned out to be great nebulae, star clusters, and even other galaxies. Messier made note of them so he wouldn't be fooled at some future time into mistaking them for his prized comets. The Messier catalog starts with M1, the Crab Nebula, and records objects up through M110, a bright galactic companion to Andromeda.

At about the same time, a more purposeful endeavor to systematically catalog deep-sky objects was made, first by British astronomer William Herschel, his sister Caroline, and later his son, John. Using a large telescope, they cataloged many thousands of deep-sky objects. This data was later organized by Danish astronomer J. L. E. Dreyer into the New General Catalogue (NGC), published in 1888. Two supplements to the NGC, called the Index Catalogues (IC), were added in 1894 and 1907. All together, the Messier, NGC, and IC catalogs contain 13,226 deep-sky objects, more than enough objects to keep a person busy for several lifetimes.

Triangulum Galaxy

AUTUMN

The Local Group

All I learn is the seasons turn, it's all I need to know.

Trevor Lucas and Pete Roche, "The Plainsman"

The autumn skies reveal the Local Group's giant spiral galaxies—Andromeda, Triangulum, and the Milky Way. In addition to the large spirals, the Local Group contains several bright irregular galaxies, several dim irregulars, several dwarf galaxies, and even a highly stripped galaxy.

Because of its proximity, the Local Group represents a unique opportunity to study galaxy evolution in great detail. Galaxies evolve by two primary methods. The first is dynamical, through the acquisition of smaller systems, mostly dwarf galaxies, into the basic structure of the parent galaxy. The second is internal, through the life cycle of stars in the spiral arms of the galaxy.

The Local Group's dominant galaxies, Andromeda and the Milky Way, have each acquired satellite galaxies. At least a dozen such satellites orbit the Milky Way, including a system of dwarf galaxies containing the Magellanic Clouds and the Sagittarius Dwarf Elliptical Galaxy, the latter of which is actively being consumed by our galaxy. Andromeda has two well-known bright companions, M32 and M110, in addition to several other lesser-known dwarf satellites. There are other members, mostly dwarf galaxies, that cannot be assigned to any particular subgroup and seem to float alone in the Local Group.

The Milky Way and Andromeda orbit each other and, as the two giants of the Local Group, comprise at least half the group's total mass. The gravitational center of the Local Group lies somewhere between the two giant spirals, and some astronomers believe the two will ultimately merge to form a giant elliptical galaxy.

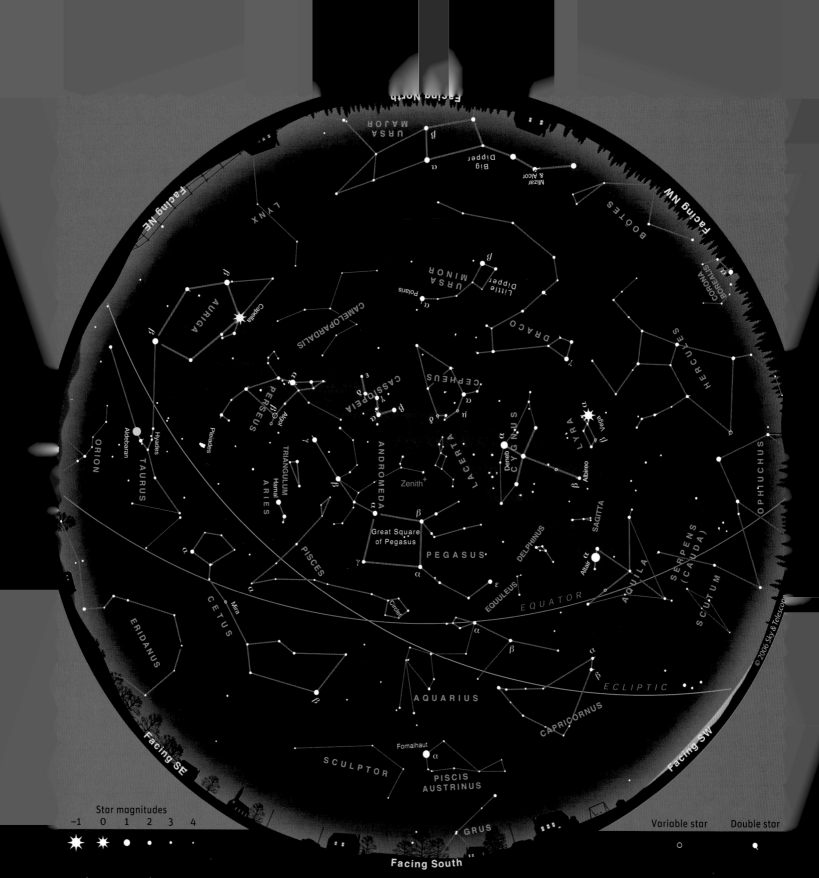

Facing North

URSA MAJOR

β

α

Big Dipper

Mizar & Alcor

BOÖTES

Facing NW

Facing NE

LYNX

β

URSA MINOR

β

Little Dipper

Polaris

α

CAMELOPARDALIS

DRACO

CORONA BOREALIS

AURIGA

Capella

β

CASSIOPEIA

ε

δ

γ

β

CEPHEUS

α

μ

δ

HERCULES

PERSEUS

Algol

β

ρ

γ

CYGNUS

LYRA

Vega

α

PLEIADES

ORION

Aldebaran

Hyades

TAURUS

Pleiades

ARIES

Hamal

TRIANGULUM

γ

β

ANDROMEDA

LACERTA

Deneb

α

β

Albireo

β

α

Zenith

Great Square
of Pegasus

β

SAGITTA

OPHIUCHUS

PISCES

α

CETUS

Mira

γ

α

PEGASUS

DELPHINUS

EQUULEUS

Altair

α

AQUILA

SERPENS
(CAUDA)

ERIDANUS

Circlet

3

α

β

EQUATOR

SCUTUM

β

ECLIPTIC

AQUARIUS

α

β

CAPRICORNUS

©2006 Sky & Telescope

Facing SE

SCULPTOR

Fomalhaut

α

PISCIS
AUSTRINUS

Facing SW

GRUS

Star magnitudes

−1 0 1 2 3 4

Variable star   Double star

Facing South

When To Use This Star Map
Early September: midnight
Late September: 11 p.m.
Early October: 10 p.m.
Late October: 9 p.m.
Early November: 8 p.m.

These are standard times. If daylight-saving time is in effect, add one hour. Use the chart within an hou
or so of the times listed. Hold the chart in front of you and turn it so the yellow label for the directio
you're facing is at the bottom, right-side up. The stars above the chart's horizon should match thos

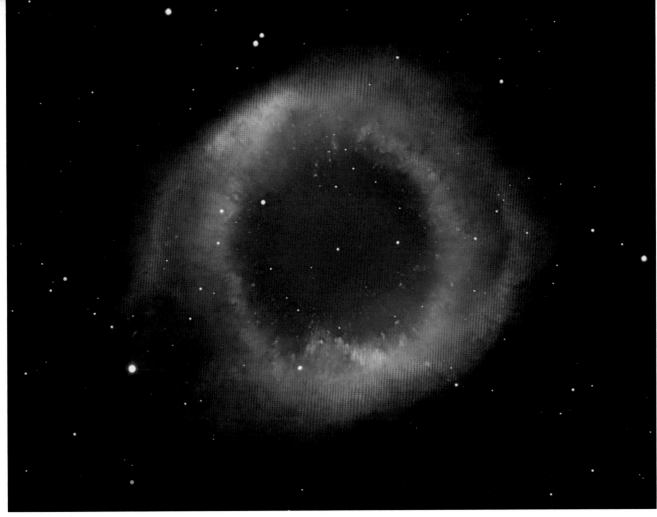

NGC 7293

HELIX NEBULA

Constellation: Aquarius. Distance: 694 light years.

Right Ascension: 22 hours : 29.6 minutes
Declination: -20 degrees : 48 minutes

The remnant of a dying star, the Helix Nebula is the nearest planetary nebula to our sun. A series of ringlike structures extends outward from the star and represent gases released during different phases of its death.

The inner ring of the nebula comprises a series of radially arranged cometary knots several trillion miles from the central star. Cometary knots, a phenomenon associated with planetary nebulae, are each several billion miles across—several times the size of our solar system. Their tails, each a hundred billion miles long, point away from the central star. The structures result from the collision of two expanding gas fronts having different temperatures and densities. The collision destabilizes the gases, resulting in the fragmentation and condensation of the gases into large droplets, which we see as the cometary heads.

M15

Also cataloged as NGC 7078. Constellation: Pegasus. Distance: 33,600 light years.

Right Ascension: 21 hours : 30.0 minutes
Declination: +12 degrees : 10 minutes

The bright globular cluster M15 packs one of the densest cores known for such a structure. As globular clusters evolve, the more massive stars, such as neutron stars, gravitate to the center. The cluster then readjusts itself in the gravitational sense. In the process of rearranging, more stars are drawn to the center, leading to an even more compact core. Although the true nature of M15's compact center is still obscure, some evidence supports the theory that it contains an intermediate-mass black hole.

Hickson 92

STEPHAN'S QUINTET

Also cataloged as Arp 319. Individual galaxies cataloged as NGC 7317, NGC 7318a, NGC 7318b, NGC 7319, NGC 7320. Constellation: Pegasus. Distance: 260 million light years, except NGC 7320.

Right Ascension: 22 hours : 35.9 minutes
Declination: +33 degrees : 57 minutes

Discovered by the French astronomer Edouard Stephan in 1877, this quintet of spiral galaxies is considered the prototype of small, compact galactic groups. Stephan initially identified five relatively bright members. In 1961, measurements of the redshift (a measure of receding velocity that can be used to estimate distance) of the group members revealed that NGC 7320, the largest, is actually receding at a slower velocity than the other four. These four are gravitationally interacting, and the interloper NGC 7320 is a foreground galaxy. The true members lie at a distance of 260 million light years, while NGC 7320 is much closer, at a distance of 50 million to 100 million light years.

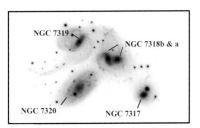

NGC 7331

Constellation: Pegasus. Distance: 50 million light years.

Right Ascension: 22 hours : 37.1 minutes
Declination: +34 degrees : 25 minutes

What does the Milky Way look like from the vast distance of 50 million light years? NGC 7331 gives us a good idea. Recent detailed observations of NGC 7331 reveal great similarities in the distribution of stars, overall mass, spiral pattern, and the likely presence of a monstrous black hole at the galactic core. These striking similarities offer an unusual outside perspective on our own galaxy.

E
Z

NGC 7380

Constellation: Cepheus. Distance: 10,400 light years.

Right Ascension: 22 hours : 47.0 minutes
Declination: +58 degrees : 06 minutes

Open star clusters are frequently born from the nebulosity that they subsequently illuminate. The ultraviolet radiation of the stars converts the parent nebula into a bright HII region that glows with the red light of fluorescing hydrogen gas. NGC 7380 is a bright open cluster of high-mass O- and B-type stars that formed four million years ago; Sh2-142 is the emission nebula, or HII region, in which the stars are embedded. The distinctive structure has interlaced bright rims and arc-shaped dust lanes. This configuration suggests that the HII region is, in essence, a blister of ionization gas positioned along the surface of its parent molecular cloud and is being viewed edge-on.

N

E

Sh2-155

CAVE NEBULA

Constellation: Cepheus. Distance: 2,900 light years.

Right Ascension: 22 hours : 58.0 minutes
Declination: +62 degrees : 34 minutes

The Cave Nebula is a brightly rimmed HII cloud where low-mass star formation is occurring. Within the spiral arms of galaxies, the most massive and luminous stars appear in groupings called OB associations, dominated by hot young blue O- and B-type stars. The stars of the Cave Nebula belong to the Cepheus OB3 association, one of the nearest OB associations to our solar system. The stars are very young, mostly less than 100,000 years old. Noticeable in the image is a small pocket of pre-main-sequence, or infant, stars glowing from within a dusty cavern of the nebula.

NGC 7635

BUBBLE NEBULA

Constellation: Cassiopeia. Distance: 7,800 light years.

Right Ascension: 23 hours : 20.7 minutes
Declination: +61 degrees : 12 minutes

Imagine a star forty times more massive and several hundred thousand times more luminous than our sun. The celestial body at the center of the Bubble Nebula is such a star. Its enormous energy output and powerful stellar winds have blown a titanic bubble of ionized gas measuring 6 light years in diameter. Popularly known as the Bubble Nebula, the strange, symmetrically round nebula is the outcome of a powerful Wolf-Rayet star. These rare stars begin their lives with at least twenty-five times the mass of our sun. Their stellar winds deplete the star's outer layers and form characteristic nebulae.

E
Z

E
Z

NGC 7822

Constellation: Cepheus. Distance: 2,750 light years.

Right Ascension: 00 hours : 03.6 minutes
Declination: +68 degrees : 37 minutes

A young stellar association of over forty massive stars illuminates this HII region. The fainter northern arch of nebulosity is designated NGC 7822, and the brighter southern cloud is designated S 171, from naval astronomer Stewart Sharpless' 1959 catalog of HII regions. The molecular cloud complex that gave rise to the visible nebula and its stars is one of the largest in the Milky Way.

The oldest stars in this stellar association formed only five million years ago. Stellar winds and supernovae-driven shock fronts produced by the association's most massive stars have blown an immense shell of molecular gas with a diameter of 200 light years.

E ← N

NGC 55

Constellation: Sculptor. Distance: 5.8 million light years.

Right Ascension: 00 hours : 14.9 minutes
Declination: -39 degrees : 11 minutes

NGC 55 is one of the nearest members of the Sculptor Group of galaxies. Considerable star formation is occurring in the galaxy's central region, where starbursts have occurred as recently as eight million years ago. Astronomers have identified large shell-like structures and plumes, signatures of massive stars and recent supernovae. A steady production of star formation has apparently occurred in NGC 55 during the last 100 million to 200 million years, suggesting a remarkably uniform star-forming history.

E

↑

└→Z

NGC 104

Also cataloged as 47 Tucanae. Constellation: Tucana. Distance: 15,650 light years.

Right Ascension: 00 hours : 24.1 minutes
Declination: -72 degrees : 05 minutes

The concentrated light of a million stars makes an impressive sight, particularly when it arises from the confines of 120 light years of space. This ultracompact light source makes 47 Tucanae, in the constellation Tucana, the second-brightest globular cluster in the sky, surpassed only by Omega Centauri in the constellation Centaurus. If Earth were placed near the center of 47 Tucanae, the collective starlight would create a nighttime as bright as day. Strong evidence exists for stellar collisions in the compact core. An enigmatic subset of blue stars known as "blue stragglers" have been identified in the overcrowded cluster core. These mysterious stars received their name because they appear to be straggling behind the evolutionary path of normal stars.

M31
ANDROMEDA GALAXY

Also cataloged as NGC 224. Constellation: Andromeda. Distance: 2.5 million light years.

Right Ascension: 00 hours: 42.7 minutes
Declination: +41 degrees : 16 minutes

M31 has played a pivotal role in astronomy. Early observers saw the soft, foggy patch of glowing light in the constellation Andromeda as just another spiral nebula. The true nature of M31 became clear in 1923. Edwin Hubble, using the newly completed 100-inch Hooker telescope at the Mount Wilson observatory, made his monumental discovery of Cepheid variable stars in M31 and, in one stroke, forever changed the astronomical paradigm of the universe. Interpreting the Cepheid data, Hubble was the first to appreciate M31 as a galaxy in its own right, similar to our Milky Way. Hubble's work opened the door to our modern interpretation of the universe, which we now know consists of countless galaxies. The Andromeda Galaxy has the distinction of being the nearest of all galaxies to our own. Its disk, tilted toward Earth by some 13 degrees, exposes the grandeur of its spiral structure and numerous star systems.

Contrary to most galaxies, which are receding from one another, Andromeda and the Milky Way are actually moving toward each other, and a close encounter—or even a full collision—may be in store in several billion years. Studies of globular clusters in the Andromeda Galaxy have revealed at least four different subpopulations, including some much younger than those that exist in the Milky Way. These findings suggest that the Andromeda Galaxy may have cannibalized numerous smaller galactic neighbors during its long and complex history. The picture below shows the core of the famous galaxy. The full galaxy can be seen on the frontispiece.

E
↑
└→ Z

NGC 247

Constellation: Cetus. Distance: 8.3 million light years.

Right Ascension: 00 hours: 47.1 minutes
Declination: -20 degrees : 46 minutes

The dwarf galaxy NGC 247 belongs to the Sculptor Group of galaxies. Small size and mass define dwarf galaxies, the most numerous galactic type in the universe. In the standard scenario of cosmic evolution, galaxies build up via the hierarchical merging of smaller galaxies. Dwarfs represent simple primordial galaxies unchanged over billions of years. As simple systems, they play a major role in large galaxy formation, serving as essential building blocks.

E
↑
└→Z

NGC 253

SCULPTOR GALAXY

Constellation: Sculptor. Distance: 12.8 million light years.

Right Ascension: 00 hours : 47.6 minutes
Declination: -25 degrees : 17 minutes

The nearest galactic group to our Local Group, the Sculptor Group is a loosely bound physical grouping of galaxies, the brightest of which is the Sculptor Galaxy. The group includes four other prominent members—NGC 55, NGC 247, NGC 300, and NGC 7793—as well as a number of dwarf galaxies. The prototypical starburst galaxy, the Sculptor Galaxy shows evidence of violent bursts of star formation in its core that began some thirty million years ago. Because the central 10,000 light years of the galaxy are cloaked in dust, astronomers use infrared instruments to understand its inner structure. Like other starburst galaxies, the Sculptor Galaxy shows evidence of a galactic "superwind" phenomenon. A massive output of energy and matter, much of it in the form of multimillion-degree plasma, streams from the center of the galaxy into the intergalactic medium. The ultrahot gases produce abundant X-ray emission. The driving force of the superwind is believed to be the collective energy outflow from episodic star birth, including shock fronts and emission released from supernovae. Galactic winds are always coupled to high levels of star formation.

NGC 281

PACMAN NEBULA

Also cataloged as S 184 and ADS 719. Constellation: Cassiopeia. Distance: 9,600 light years.

Right Ascension: 00 hours : 52.8 minutes
Declination: +56 degrees : 37 minutes

The Pacman Nebula is a classic HII cloud illuminated by its progeny of young stars. Located in the Perseus spiral arm of our galaxy, the visible structure spans some 60 light years. The molecular cloud from which the emission nebula arose has been busy in the last few million years forming the massive young stars of the central cluster IC 1590 (just above center). The energy source for the nebula, IC 1590 is an excellent example of a young open cluster abundant with infant stars, indicating ongoing star formation.

Several compact dark structures known as Bok globules are projected against the background of the nebula. These structures, first described by astronomer Bart Bok in the 1940s, are small dark clouds of gas and dust typically found in HII regions. Infrared observations in the 1990s detected protostars within the dense confines of these globules, confirming Bok's hypothesis that they represent cocoons of star birth. The largest Bok globule in the Pacman Nebula is about 2.6 light years in diameter.

NGC 300

Constellation: Sculptor. Distance: 6.5 million light years.

Right Ascension: 00 hours: 54.9 minutes
Declination: -37 degrees : 41 minutes

A bright spiral similar to the Triangulum Galaxy, NGC 300 belongs to the nearby Sculptor Group of galaxies. Because of its proximity and nearly face-on orientation, much is known about NGC 300. Among other things, NGC 300 has been the subject of exhaustive searches for extragalactic Wolf-Rayet stars. Over a dozen candidates for this rare, powerful star have been identified.

Gamma Cassiopeiae

Constellation: Cassiopeia. Distance: 600 light years.

Right Ascension: 00 hours : 56.7 minutes
Declination: +61 degrees : 04 minutes

Gamma Cassiopeiae, a bright variable star in the constellation Cassiopeia, forms a triangle with the comet-shaped nebulae IC 59 and IC 63. The intense radiation pressure of Gamma Cas, which likely sculpted the cometary shape of the two nebulae, serves as the prime source of their illumination. Gamma Cas belongs to a special group of variable stars called Be stars. In fact, Gamma Cas was the very first Be star discovered. Be stars are massive O-type stars distinguished by rapid rotation, up to 150 times faster than our own sun. The rotation causes substantial variability in brightness and concentrates the stellar winds within the star's disk. At 70,000 times the brightness of our sun, the enormous luminosity and winds of Gamma Cas conspire to drive mass from the star. The periodic mass outflows are typically followed by visual dimming of the star. Between 1935 and 1940, Gamma Cas varied in brightness from 1.6 to 3.0 and significantly changed the appearance of the constellation Cassiopeia.

Z ←
↓
E

NGC 292

SMALL MAGELLANIC CLOUD

Constellation: Tucana. Distance: 163,000 light years.

Right Ascension: 00 hours : 52.8 minutes
Declination: -72 degrees : 50 minutes

The Large and Small Magellanic Clouds are a pair of dwarf irregular galaxies that orbit the Milky Way. Similar to other dwarf irregulars, they are rich in gas and dust and exhibit higher-than-normal levels of active star formation. Cherry red emission clouds and clusters of massive young blue stars are testament to the active star formation going on in the Small Magellanic Cloud. The Magellanic Clouds and the Milky Way have a long history of mutual interaction that has profoundly affected the structure and star-forming history of all three galaxies. Galaxy evolution is a complex, multi-factorial process, with star formation as one of the supreme driving forces.

M33

TRIANGULUM GALAXY

Also cataloged as NGC 598. Constellation: Triangulum. Distance: 2.4 million light years.

Right Ascension: 01 hours : 33.9 minutes
Declination: +30 degrees : 39 minutes

Star-forming HII regions populate the broad spiral arms of the Triangulum Galaxy, the third largest member of our Local Group. Only Andromeda and the Milky Way are larger. The Triangulum Galaxy's face-on orientation and proximity allow detailed study of its HII clouds. Some of the less-distinct HII regions are not associated with star clusters and are

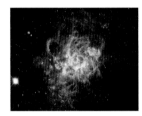

probably illuminated by an ultraviolet flux radiating throughout much of the spiral arm structure. Some shell-like nebulae represent enormous bubbles blown by powerful stellar winds and supernovae. The brightest and most impressive HII region in Triangulum is NGC 604 (left). This massive nebula spans 1,600 light years, distinguishing it as one of the largest known HII regions.

E
Z

E
→Z

M74

Also cataloged as NGC 628. Constellation: Pisces. Distance: 32 million light years.

Right Ascension: 01 hours : 36.7 minutes
Declination: +15 degrees : 47 minutes

The prototypical "grand design" spiral galaxy, M74 possesses two exquisitely symmetric spiral arms. Its face-on position gives observers a dramatic view of these arms. Studies at ultraviolet wavelengths provide evidence of a higher-than-normal level of star formation that has occurred at a fairly steady rate over the last 500 million years. The galaxy's abundant HII regions are directly related to this prolonged epoch of star formation.

M76
LITTLE DUMBBELL NEBULA

Also cataloged as NGC 650-1 and popularly known as the Cork Nebula or the Butterfly Nebula.
Constellation: Perseus. Distance: 3,900 light years.

Right Ascension: 01 hours : 42.3 minutes
Declination: +51 degrees : 34 minutes

The Little Dumbbell Nebula is a stunning example of a bipolar planetary nebula. A fairly evolved nebula, it likely formed more than ten thousand years ago. The basic structure is a complex napkin-ring-shaped core with two attached inner lobes and two fainter outer lobes. In the current model of planetary nebula formation, the progenitor star loses a considerable amount of mass in its final stage. The resulting superwind blows gases primarily into an equatorial plane, producing the characteristic bi-lobed configuration. Ultimately, the core of the dying star becomes exposed and its hot, fast wind collides with the equatorial-shaped envelope of gas, expanding it into a bipolar shape.

The Little Dumbbell Nebula stretches about 4.5 light years across and its hot central stellar remnant is about 140,000 degrees Kelvin.

NGC 884 and NGC 869

DOUBLE CLUSTER

Also cataloged as h and Chi Persei. Constellation: Perseus. Distance: 7,500 light years.

Right Ascension: 02 hours : 22.4 minutes
Declination: +57 degrees : 07 minutes

A renowned pair of open star clusters, NGC 884 (left) and NGC869 (right), also known as the Double Cluster, reside in the Perseus arm of the Milky Way. The clusters count among the brightest, densest, and closest of the open clusters containing moderately massive stars. Only a few hundred light years separate the two clusters, which probably form the core of the immense stellar association Perseus OB1. Many of its members are hot and luminous O- and B-type giants, some shining sixty thousand times brighter than our sun. The strikingly similar clusters are believed to have originated from a single ancestral cloud some 12.8 million years ago.

N
E

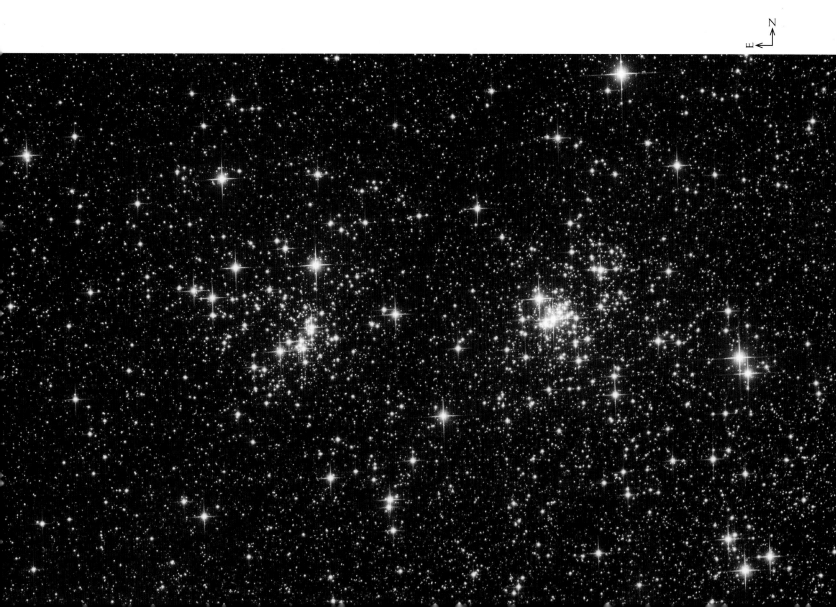

NGC 891

Constellation: Andromeda. Distance: 8.9 million light years.

Right Ascension: 02 hours : 22.6 minutes
Declination: +42 degrees : 21 minutes

The equatorial disk of a spiral galaxy is never so apparent as when viewed edge-on. NGC 891, inclined 88.3 degrees, allows an appreciation of the disk's exceedingly thin and flat nature and its dense, dusty contents. Extraplanar dust structures distinguish NGC 891. These huge filaments of dust align perpendicular to the disk and extend above and below as far as 7,200 light years from the galaxy's central plane. At higher galactic latitudes, some of the dust filaments assume a peculiar parallel alignment with the galactic plane. Some of the more prominent filaments contain some 100,000 solar masses of material.

E

Z

IC 1848, IC 1805, and IC 1795

HEART AND SOUL NEBULAE

Constellation: Cassiopeia. Distance: 7,500 light years.

Right Ascension: 02 hours : 32.7 minutes
Declination: +61 degrees : 27 minutes

Among some of the best-known star-forming regions in the Milky Way is a chain of HII clouds (IC 1848, IC 1805, and IC 1795 from left to right) known as the Heart and Soul Nebulae, located in the Perseus arm. Massive O- and B-type stars, as seen in the close up of IC1848 (right), illuminate these glowing emission clouds. Young massive stars in these regions have triggered bursts of new star formation as the giant molecular clouds they illuminate expand into and compress the surrounding denser gaseous medium.

Melotte 15

Constellation: Cassiopeia. Distance: 7,500 light years.

Right Ascension: 02 hours : 32.7 minutes
Declination: +61 degrees : 27 minutes

At the center of IC 1805 is the young open cluster also known as Melotte 15. Object number 15 in the catalog of star clusters by the British-Belgian astronomer Philibert Jacques Melotte (1880–1961) is an extremely young cluster of massive OB stars with a mean age of only 1.5 million years. It is one of the core clusters of the Cas OB6 association and is positioned some 50 light years in front of the nebula. It is itself associated with substantial nebulosity.

M34

Also cataloged as NGC 1039. Constellation: Perseus. Distance: 1,500 light years.

Right Ascension: 02 hours: 42.0 minutes
Declination: +42 degrees : 47 minutes

Although often overlooked for its famous neighbor, the Double Cluster, M34 is a beautiful open cluster in its own right, spanning about 10 light years. At some 250 million years old, its hundred or so members are middle-aged for an open cluster. The more massive white and blue stars stand out among their lower-mass brethren. A few cluster members have left the main sequence and are conspicuous as red giants.

E
Z

M77

Also cataloged as NGC 1068. Constellation: Cetus. Distance: 50 million light years.

Right Ascension: 02 hours : 42.7 minutes
Declination: -00 degrees : 01 minutes

M77 is the prototypical Seyfert galaxy and the brightest of its class. Galaxies of this type are named for the American astronomer Carl K. Seyfert, who in 1943 described their characteristics, namely a brilliant starlike nucleus, faint spiral arms, and specific emission line spectra from their nucleus. M77 is a large galaxy and, together with its faint outer arms, may extend 170,000 light years across. Seyfert galaxies, like other active galaxies, are believed to have a supermassive black hole as their central engine. The very compact, highly luminous nucleus of Seyfert galaxies can literally outshine the remainder of the parent galaxy.

Abell 426

PERSEUS CLUSTER

Constellation: Perseus. Distance: 230 million light years.

Right Ascension: 03 hours : 19.8 minutes
Declination: +41 degrees : 31 minutes

The rich Perseus Cluster of galaxies contains more than five hundred members, centered around the large elliptical galaxy NGC 1275 (upper right). Among galaxy clusters, the Perseus Cluster emits the brightest X-ray emission known, arising from immense gravitational forces at the center of the cluster that crush the existing diffuse gas to high density and temperatures of up to 100 million degrees Kelvin.

In 1958, the American astronomer George O. Abell compiled an extensive catalog of galaxy clusters. The final catalog, completed posthumously in 1987, includes approximately four thousand clusters. Among these is the Perseus-Pisces Supercluster, of which the Perseus Cluster dominates. The supercluster forms a dense wall of galaxies that extends across 300 million light years and some 40 degrees of sky.

The Perseus-Pisces Supercluster is one of two dominant concentrations of galaxies on either side of our Local Supercluster. On one side is a dense concentration of galaxies and dark matter called the Great Attractor, which appears to be pulling the Local Supercluster in its direction at a velocity of 600 kilometers per second. In the opposite direction, and also in line with our galactic plane, the almost equally massive Perseus-Pisces Supercluster exerts its own enormous gravitational pull. The outcome of these competing megastructures is a cosmic tug of war with our Local Supercluster in the center and the eventual winner still uncertain.

NGC 1333

Constellation: Perseus. Distance: 720 light years.

Right Ascension: 03 hours : 29.3 minutes
Declination: +31 degrees : 25 minutes

The diverse nebula NGC 1333 formed from a molecular cloud complex in the Perseus arm of our galaxy. It is one of the nearest star-forming regions and is particularly rich in infant stars. During their early evolution, stars are heavily obscured by dust, rendering them invisible to optical instruments. They are often detectable only at infrared wavelengths. Also, several bright Herbig-Haro objects (glowing red patches) have been identified in NGC 1333, confirming its status as an active region of star formation. Herbig-Haro objects, named after astronomers George Herbig and Guillermo Haro, are small emission nebulae produced by the energetic outflows of young stellar objects during the first few hundred thousand years of life.

NGC 1365

Constellation: Fornax. Distance: 61 million light years.

Right Ascension: 03 hours : 33.6 minutes
Declination: -36 degrees: 08 minutes

NGC 1365 is a true giant of the sky. Rivaled only by M101 in the Local Group, the symmetric spiral structure spans 200,000 light years. NGC 1365 is the prototypical barred galaxy with an active galactic nucleus belonging to the subclass of Seyfert galaxies. NGC 1365's nuclear region releases intense energy thought to arise from a supermassive black hole. Typical of galaxies with an AGN, a bidirectional jet of superheated plasma is expelled from the galaxy's nuclear region at speeds close to the speed of light.

Orion Nebula

WINTER

Clouds of Creation

*Time goes by so slowly
and time can do so much.*

—Bill Medley and Bobby Hatfield

Deep-sky observers wait in excited anticipation for the cold, clear skies of winter—the season of brilliant and beautiful nebulae. Vast flowing clouds of fantastic forms and brilliant colors await us during these months. The best introduction to the winter sky is the fabulous region of Orion, one of the great regions of active star formation in our galaxy. Its proximity and favorable position in the sky have made this one of the most extensively studied regions in the Milky Way. Three prime components make up the Orion star-forming region: (1) the giant Orion molecular cloud, which has served as the repository of raw materials for forming stars in the last twelve million years, (2) the Orion OB1 stellar association, containing the young, hot stars formed from the Orion molecular cloud complex, and (3) the assortment of fantastic HII regions that populate the region, such as the Orion Nebula and the Horsehead Nebula. These colorful HII clouds have formed as thin blisters of glowing gases over the surface of their parent molecular clouds, illuminated by young massive stars.

The illuminating power of the rich nebulosity in the Orion region comes from the stars of the Orion OB1 association, which formed over the last 10 to 12 million years. Star formation has progressed in an orderly manner from the belt region of Orion to the sword region. The stars of the Orion Nebula and the nebula NGC 1977 belong to the youngest subgroup of the Orion OB association and are less than two million years old.

IC 342

Constellation: Camelopardalis. Distance: 6.5 million light years.

Right Ascension: 03 hours : 46.8 minutes
Declination: +68 degrees : 06 minutes

At its relatively close distance of 6.5 million light years, IC 342 would shine as one of the brightest galaxies in the sky if not for its untoward location. Its home is only 10.5 degrees from the disk plane, or galactic equator, of the Milky Way. Obscured by interstellar matter, its light is heavily attenuated before it reaches us. Numerous HII regions appear as prominent red dots along IC 342's faint, extended spiral arms. They are likely more visible due to the relative extinction of shorter wavelengths (blue light) by the intervening dust.

N
E ←↑

M45

PLEIADES

Also cataloged as NGC 1435 and popularly known as Subaru or the Seven Sisters. Constellation: Taurus. Distance: 435 light years.

Right Ascension: 03 hours : 47.0 minutes
Declination: +24 degrees : 07 minutes

Serendipity has created a magnificent astronomical spectacle in the Pleiades. Usually stars and their surrounding clouds are intimately related, the stars having formed from the cloud many years earlier. In the case of the Pleiades, a true galactic vagrant, the stars simply wandered into the interior of an unrelated molecular cloud. The rich blue clouds and delicate tendrils of reflection nebulosity have their origin in innumerable tiny dust particles that reflect the blue light of the embedded stars.

The proximity of this great cluster allows a close-up view of a young open cluster and the fascinating interplay of moving stars and the interstellar medium. The Pleiades moves through space at about 40 kilometers per second. The relative tightness of the cluster indicates its young age, likely some 100 million years. The bright stars of the Pleiades will probably travel through space as a bound cluster for another 250 million years before the gravity of the Milky Way breaks the cluster into individual field stars.

N
E ←

NGC 1499

CALIFORNIA NEBULA

Constellation: Perseus. Distance: 1,140 light years.

Right Ascension: 04 hours : 00.7 minutes
Declination: +36 degrees : 37 minutes

The bright emission cloud known as the California Nebula stretches across 4 degrees of winter sky. Its familiar geographic form can be found along the northern border of the Perseus OB2 stellar association. The sole source of ionizing energy of the large cloud is the bright star Xi Persei (lower right). This star has a fascinating history. While most ionizing stars form from the molecular cloud they in turn illuminate, Xi Persei belongs to a class called runaway stars. These massive O- and B-type giants have been ejected from their place of origin and travel through space interacting with various clouds. Xi Persei is believed to have originated in the Perseus OB2 stellar association some 400,000 years ago. It encountered the California Nebula as recently as 100,000 years ago.

The origin of runaway stars is controversial. One proposed scenario is that the roaming star was once the binary companion of another star that erupted as a supernova, sending its companion into space at high velocity. A competing theory is that close gravitational encounters during the early phase of cluster formation, when stellar number densities are high, led to the ejection of the individual star.

IC 2118

WITCH HEAD NEBULA

Constellation: Eridanus. Distance: 700 light years.

Right Ascension: 05 hours : 06.9 minutes
Declination: -07 degrees : 13 minutes

The bright star Rigel illuminates the Witch Head Nebula, a classic reflection nebula located 2 degrees northwest of the B-type supergiant star. The windblown appearance and cometary shape of the bright reflection cloud suggest a relationship with the high-mass luminous stars of the Orion OB1 association. The heads of the cometary clouds point northeast toward the association, supporting the theory that the association's stellar winds and radiation have sculpted the nebula into the shape we see today.

E
N

IC 405

FLAMING STAR NEBULA

Constellation: Auriga. Distance: 1,500 light years.

Right Ascension: 05 hours : 16.2 minutes
Declination: +34 degrees : 16 minutes

First discovered in 1892, the nebula complex IC 405 was described by the astronomer Max Wolf as "a burning body from which several enormous curved flames seem to break out like gigantic prominences." Wolf's famous quote led to the adoption of the popular name Flaming Star Nebula.

The Flaming Star Nebula would be invisible if not for the ionizing energy of a brilliant O-type star, AE Aurigae. Many nebulae have a single hot, massive star as their ionizing source. These stars are usually born from the raw materials of the gaseous clouds they now illuminate. Not so with AE Aurigae. The turbulent history of this star began 2.5 million years ago, when a close encounter between two massive stars occurred near the Trapezium cluster of the Orion Nebula. This collision ejected two runaway stars into space at remarkable speed. One of these stars is AE Aurigae, which continues to soar through space at 200 kilometers per second. In its travels from the Orion region, it encountered the interstellar cloud of gas and dust we know now as the Flaming Star Nebula.

LARGE MAGELLANIC CLOUD

Constellation: Dorado. Distance: 163,000 light years.

Right Ascension: 05 hours : 23.6 minutes
Declination -69 degrees : 45 minutes

Named for the explorer Ferdinand Magellan, who noted their presence in 1519, the Magellanic Clouds are a pair of dwarf irregular galaxies. They are part of the "Magellanic Stream," a long trail of tidal debris that orbits the Milky Way. The larger of the two systems, the Large Magellanic Cloud (LMC) measures some 20,000 light years across, making it the fourth largest member of the Local Group. The LMC is the second nearest neighboring galaxy to the Milky Way. It is full of remarkable objects, including the giant HII region 30 Doradus. In 1987, a supernova occurred in the LMC—the nearest observed supernova since the invention of the telescope. Massive sequential and triggered star formations occur on a large scale in the LMC. In addition to a diverse population of young stars and HII regions, the galaxy shows various warps, rings, and tidal features, all indicators of remote and recent encounters with the Milky Way.

The LMC has played an important role in astronomical research. It has served critical roles in establishing the extragalactic distance scale, understanding the astrophysics of giant HII regions and super star clusters, and advancing the knowledge of our own galaxy's history, mass, and dark matter content.

M1

CRAB NEBULA

Also cataloged as NGC 1952. Constellation: Taurus. Distance: 6,300 light years.

> Right Ascension: 05 hours : 34.5 minutes
> Declination: +22 degrees : 01 minutes

The Crab Nebula represents the remains of a shattered supergiant star that met its explosive end in the year 1054. Chinese astronomers documented the star to be four times brighter than Venus (the brightest object in the sky aside from the sun and moon) and visible in the daytime sky for twenty-three days. It is the most famous and studied supernova remnant and one of only a few observed supernovae in our own galaxy. Astronomers estimate that supernovae occur about once every three decades in the Milky Way, but dense interstellar matter obscures large parts of the galaxy, making observations much less frequent.

In 1968, a pulsating radio source was identified at the heart of the Crab Nebula, which we now identify as the Crab Pulsar, a neutron star rotating at thirty revolutions per second. The star's incredible density approaches fifty trillion times that of lead.

M42

ORION NEBULA

Also cataloged as NGC 1976. Constellation: Orion. Distance: 1,500 light years.

Right Ascension: 05 hours : 35.4 minutes
Declination: -05 degrees : 27 minutes

A recurring theme of upheaval and destruction, birth and rebirth occurs within the spiral arms of galaxies. With a gaseous repository of ten thousand suns and illuminated by a cluster of hot young stars, the clouds of the Orion Nebula give us a bird's-eye view of one of the greatest star-forming nurseries in our part of the galaxy. Glowing with fantastic colors and shapes, the Orion Nebula is arguably the greatest of all observable HII clouds.

A complex cloud of glowing gas, the Orion Nebula comprises mostly hydrogen but also helium, carbon, nitrogen, and oxygen. The nebula is essentially a bright condensation of the Orion A Molecular Cloud, which extends far beyond the nebula itself. Although it spans 40 light years, the ionized gas of the Orion Nebula forms an exceptionally thin blister only 0.08 light years thick on the surface of the larger, invisible molecular cloud.

Directly in front of the Orion Nebula is a grouping of hot O- and B-type stars known as the Trapezium, which shine between magnitude 5 and 8. This grouping represents the four brightest members of an extended cluster of several thousand young stars, many of which lie unseen within the opaque gas and dust. The bright Trapezium represents the cluster core, where stars are packed so tightly they exceed the stellar concentration of our sun's vicinity by some 20,000 times.

The Orion Nebula would be invisible if not for the Trapezium. The four stars, also called the Theta-1 group, all contribute energy to the massive nebula; however, Theta-1 C contributes the most prodigiously, supplying more than 99 percent of the ultraviolet energy. Theta-1 C is an enormous O-type giant with a surface temperature of 40,000 degrees Kelvin. Amazingly, Theta-1 C is 210,000 times more luminous than our sun and produces a gargantuan stellar wind 100,000 times the flow rate of our sun. Theta-1 C will, in all likelihood, meet its fate as a supernova in a few million years.

NGC 1977

Constellation: Orion. Distance: 1,460 light years.

Right Ascension: 05 hours : 35.5 minutes
Declination: -04 degrees : 52 minutes

Although cataloged as an HII region, NGC 1977 actually comprises a complex assortment of emission, reflection, and dust clouds. The stars of NGC 1977 are among the youngest members of the Orion OB1 stellar association. The numerous low-mass stars and infant protostars formed very recently, between two million and four million years ago, and represent the most recent episode of star birth in the Orion Nebula complex.

NGC 1999

Constellation: Orion. Distance: 1,500 light years.

Right Ascension: 05 hours : 36.5 minutes
Declination: -06 degrees : 42 minutes

The lone star V380 Orionis illuminates the classic reflection nebula NGC 1999, located about 2 degrees south of the Orion Nebula. The nebula is notable for a T-shaped Bok globule that lies in its foreground (right). The central star and the nebula have identical spectrums, which tell us that what we see is truly reflected starlight. The blue light we see is scattered by microscopic dust grains. The blue light has a similar wavelength as the dust particles and is therefore scattered more efficiently than the longer wavelengths of light.

Two bright Herbig-Haro objects exist nearby NGC 1999. They are designated HH-1 and HH-2 (seen below NGC 1999) and represent the first of these objects recognized around 1950. The nature of these objects was unknown to Herbig and Haro at the time they cataloged them. We now know they represent small nebulae energized by the outflows of nearby infant stars.

30 Doradus

TARANTULA NEBULA

Also cataloged as NGC 2070. Constellation: Dorado. Distance: 163,000 light years.

> Right Ascension: 05 hours : 38.6 minutes
> Declination: -69 degrees : 05 minutes

The largest and brightest giant HII region in our Local Group, the Tarantula Nebula stretches across a staggering 3,000 light years and has the mass of one million suns. It resides in the Large Magellanic Cloud and is the nearest extragalactic giant HII region. Because of its proximity, the Tarantula Nebula serves as a virtual laboratory of massive star formation.

The central cluster R136 provides almost half the ionizing energy within the Tarantula Nebula. R136 is an exceptional cluster by any standard. Although thousands of massive O- and B-type stars are scattered throughout the Tarantula Nebula, R136 contains an unusual number of massive giants, including several powerful Wolf-Rayet stars. The brightest star in R136, a Wolf-Rayet, has a mass of 133 suns!

The striking honeycomb appearance of the Tarantula Nebula lacks a clear counterpart in our Milky Way. The unique form suggests a series of interlocking giant shells and hollow cavities. The shells are believed to have formed from the collective stellar winds of successive generations of powerful stars and their supernovae. Astronomers estimate that the complex has experienced at least forty supernovae in the last ten thousand years.

B33 and NGC 2023

HORSEHEAD NEBULA

Constellation: Orion. Distance: 1,500 light years.

Right Ascension: 05 hours : 41.6 minute
Declination: -02 degrees : 14 minutes

Earthly dust may seem trivial, but the cosmic kind is an all-important constituent of matter in the universe and is essential to the star-making process. The famous Horsehead Nebula (B33) represents a dark cloud of dust and nonluminous gas that obscures and silhouettes the emitted light of IC 434 behind it. Protruding from its parental cloud, the Horsehead is a dynamic structure and a fascinating laboratory of complex physics. As it expands into the surrounding environment, areas of the cloud undergo stresses that trigger the formation of low-mass stars. One infant star is visible as a partly shrouded glow in the horse's brow. Small reddish objects glowing through the dust represent Herbig-Haro objects. The Barnard Catalog of Dark Nebulae was compiled by the American astronomer Edward E. Barnard and completed in the early twentieth century. The catalog has over three hundred entries, including the most famous, B33.

NGC 2023 is one of the brightest reflection nebulae in the sky and is located just northeast of the Horsehead. The central star of the blue nebula is responsible for most of the excitation of gas and dust within NGC 2023. The star is embedded within a thick dust cloud; however, its blue light penetrates through and is reflected from the surface of microscopic particles present in the cloud. A unique feature of NGC 2023 is the presence of a shell of neutral hydrogen surrounding the central star out to a radius of about 0.65 light years. The shell amazingly emits red light by a unique process called vibrational fluorescence. It is the first reflection nebula known to exhibit this type of phenomenon.

E ← ↓N

NGC 2024

FLAME NEBULA

Constellation: Orion. Distance: 1,500 light years.

Right Ascension: 05 hours : 41.9 minutes
Declination: -01 degrees : 51 minutes

Although the bright blue light of the supergiant star Alnitak threatens to overwhelm the Flame Nebula, the two are not physically related. The flamelike nebula is a bright HII region on the surface of the Orion B molecular cloud complex 1,500 light years away. Alnitak, on the other hand, is several hundred light years in the foreground.

The Flame Nebula's bifurcated dusty structure is mostly opaque to optical telescopes. Infrared telescopes have penetrated the dusty veil and discovered a rich cluster of stars all younger than one million years. At least half the stars are encircled by dusty disks known as accretion disks, possibly the precursors of terrestrial earthlike planets.

Simeis 147

Also cataloged as Sh2-240. Constellation: Taurus. Distance: 3,900 light years.

Right Ascension: 05 hours : 43.12 minutes
Declination +28 degrees : 17 minutes

Simeis 147 is a large mature supernova remnant in the constellation Taurus. Although long thought to be almost 100,000 years old, more recent data indicate a younger estimate of about thirty thousand years. S147 spans 100 light years and is expanding at 1,000 kilometers per second. The supernova left behind a pulsar, spinning at about seven times per second.

E
↑
└→Z

M78

Also cataloged as NGC 2068. Constellation: Orion. Distance: 1,300 light years.

Right Ascension: 05 hours : 46.7 minutes
Declination: +00 degrees : 03 minutes

The bright reflection nebula M78 spans 4 light years across the Orion B molecular cloud. The complex includes the prominent reflection nebula NGC 2071 (upper right), among several others. Infrared studies have discovered many low-mass stars in the region. Some of these nascent stars exhibit dramatic Herbig-Haro outflow phenomenon, indicators of stars in their formative stages.

In February 2004, the amateur astronomer Julian McNeil discovered a variable nebula, visible in the lower left of the image. A young star located at the nebula's apex illuminates the fan-shaped cloud. The rare phenomenon of variable nebulae is most likely explained by mass being absorbed by a forming star, which induces transient brightening of the star and subsequent energizing of nearby gas clouds.

Mon R2 Association

Constellation: Monoceros. Distance: 2,700 light years.

Right Ascension: 06 hours : 07.5 minutes
Declination: -06 degrees : 24 minutes

A magical display of exuberant reflection and emission nebulosity exists in the western part of a vast star-forming region known as the Mon R2 association in the constellation Monoceros. The "R" designation stands for reflection and indicates an association of stars illuminating reflection nebulae. The association of B-type stars formed about six million to ten million years ago, along the edge of the Mon R2 molecular cloud. The Canadian astronomer Sidney Van den Bergh identified this clustering in his 1966 catalog of over 150 reflection nebulae, or VdB objects. The core of the Mon R2 molecular cloud is associated with several radio-wave sources thought to originate from water, formaldehyde, and hydroxyl MASERs (Microwave Amplification by Stimulated Emission of Radiation). MASERs form in very active star-forming regions through the interaction of high-energy starlight with regions rich in complex molecules.

M35 and NGC 2158

M35 also cataloged as NGC 2168. Constellation: Gemini.
Distance to M35: 2,700 light years. Distance to NGC 2158: 15,000 light years.

Right Ascension: 06 hours : 08.9 minutes
Declination: +24 degrees : 20 minutes

Although the photograph suggests proximity, in reality a great distance separates the open clusters M35 and NGC 2158, and their stellar populations could not be more different. M35, at the upper left of the photograph, is 2,700 light years away, while NGC 2158 is much more distant, at around 15,000 light years.

Close inspection reveals disparities in star color that underscore the two clusters' different histories. The clusters probably came into being with similar populations—mostly blue and white massive O- and B-types with some lower-mass yellow and orange types. M35, comparatively young at 95 million years old, still maintains an abundance of blue and white massive stars. Even in this short time period, however, some red giants have evolved, hinting at the fate of the cluster's other stars. In contrast, NGC 2158 is over a billion years old, enough time to lose its O- and B-types to supernovae. All that remain in NGC 2158 are the lower-mass, older orange and yellow suns.

Most open clusters are loosely bound by gravity and eventually disperse after a few hundred million years. NGC 2158 is more compact than most clusters of its age, indicating that gravity has had a tighter grip on the individual stars and allowed it to become an unusual ancient cluster.

E ← N (compass indicator, lower left of image)

IC 443

JELLYFISH NEBULA

Constellation: Gemini. Distance: 5,000 light years.

Right Ascension: 06 hours : 16.9 minutes
Declination: +22 degrees : 47 minutes

The Jellyfish Nebula is an unusual occurrence of a supernova remnant interacting with a molecular cloud. A great supernova detonated in the constellation Gemini, leaving in its wake a shell of heated gas that expanded into the interstellar medium and ultimately collided with a large molecular cloud. Much of the red light represents ionization of the gases in the molecular cloud. Astronomers recently identified a neutron star at the center of the Jellyfish Nebula, the fossil remnant of the dying star that set events in motion some thirty thousand years ago.

E ← ↓ N

NGC 2237, NGC 2238, NGC 2239, and NGC 2246

ROSETTE NEBULA

Constellation: Monoceros. Distance: 5,000 light years.

Right Ascension: 06 hours : 32.4 minutes
Declination: +04 degrees : 52 minutes

Arguably one of the finest HII regions in the northern sky, the Rosette Nebula covers approximately 130 light years and contains enough gas and dust to make ten thousand stars. The center of the nebula contains a young open cluster, NGC 2244, composed of O- and B-type giant stars. The radiation pressure and powerful stellar winds of these massive stars have excavated the center of the Rosette and provide the excitation for the wreathlike emission cloud. The winds impart momentum to the cloud's ambient gas, expanding the nebula at about 4 kilometers per second.

NGC 2261

HUBBLE'S VARIABLE NEBULA

Constellation: Monoceros. Distance: 2,500 light years.

Right Ascension: 06 hours : 39.2 minutes
Declination: +08 degrees : 44 minutes

The young star R Monocerotis and its fan-shaped reflection nebula NGC 2261 represent one of the most thoroughly investigated star-and-nebula systems in the last hundred years. The hollow, conical-shaped nebula has been observed since the times of Sir William Herschel, and the illuminating source at its base has been known as a variable star for almost 150 years, fluctuating by as much as four magnitudes in brightness. In 1916, Edwin Hubble found that the nebula could vary on a time scale of months and it has since been known as Hubble's Variable Nebula. The rapid changes in nebula brightness are shadows cast by dusty matter orbiting R Mon.

NGC 2264

CHRISTMAS TREE
CLUSTER

Constellation: Monoceros. Distance: 2,600 light years.

Right Ascension: 06 hours : 41.1 minutes
Declination: +09 degrees : 53 minutes

The young star cluster NGC 2264 resides in the Orion arm of our galaxy. It contains over six hundred stars ranging in age from one million to four million years. The brightest members resemble a Christmas tree, with the Cone Nebula at its apex and the star S Monocerotis at its base. Dark dust clouds and glowing gas have carved out the striking landscape we see in the Cone Nebula. The conical-shaped pillar of gas and dust spans about 7 light years. S Monocerotis dominates the northern half of the Christmas Tree Cluster and probably provides the ionizing source of the Cone Nebula. An O-type supergiant and the most massive stellar member of the cluster, S Monocerotis is about eight thousand times more luminous than our sun.

N← →
E↓

IC 2177

SEAGULL NEBULA

Constellation: Monoceros. Distance: 1,800 light years.

Right Ascension: 07 hours : 05.1 minutes
Declination: -10 degrees : 42 minutes

The bright HII region on the border of the constellations Monoceros and Canis Major suggests the image of a bird or, more specifically, a seagull. The complex to which the Seagull Nebula belongs consists of mostly emission nebulae scattered with blue reflection nebulae and dark dust clouds. The "head" of the seagull is designated as NGC 2327 (right). The bright HII region is about one million years old and has two prominent embedded clusters, NGC 2335 and NGC 2343. The two clusters are thought to represent a double cluster of common origin, similar to the famous Double Cluster in the constellation Perseus.

NGC 2359

THOR'S HELMET

Also popularly known as the Duck Nebula. Constellation: Canis Major. Distance: 15,000 light years.

Right Ascension: 07 hours : 18.6 minutes
Declination: -13 degrees : 12 minutes

Although NGC 2359 may seem like an ethereal and peaceful object, its outward appearance hides the violent processes that gave rise to the peculiar nebula known as Thor's Helmet. Fierce stellar winds, shed by an extremely massive and unstable Wolf-Rayet star, created the bubble-shaped filamentary nebula. These types of stars have become unstable in the late stages of their short stellar life and heavily influence the surrounding interstellar medium.

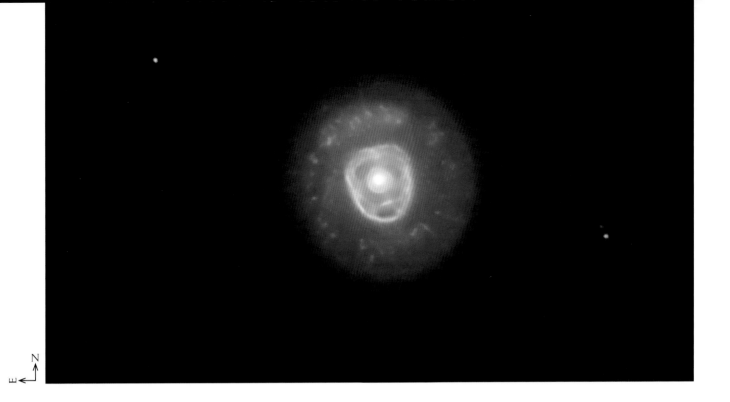

E ← N

NGC 2392

ESKIMO NEBULA

Also popularly known as the Clown Face Nebula. Constellation: Gemini. Distance: 2,900 light years.

Right Ascension: 07 hours : 29.2 minutes
Declination: +20 degrees : 55 minutes

The bright planetary nebula known as the Eskimo Nebula has a conspicuous double-ring structure. The unique forms assumed by planetary nebulae tell a story of mass loss and subsequent shaping by the dynamical processes of the parent star. In attempting to explain these puzzling shapes, astronomers have created three-dimensional models of planetary nebulae from two-dimensional images with increasing success.

The general structure of the Eskimo Nebula is a double shell with inner and outer components surrounding its central star. The once low-mass star has entered its final stages as a compact collapsed white dwarf with a surface temperature of 40,000 degrees Kelvin, about forty times more luminous than our sun. It no longer shines by way of nuclear fusion. Instead, the radiation of the central star superheats the gases in the inner shell to temperatures up to 2 million degrees, causing the emission of high-energy X-rays. The inner shell is a young structure less than a thousand years old. The outer shell is composed predominantly of doubly ionized oxygen and older gases more than five thousand years old.

The cometary filaments and knots of the outer regions formed from the collision of two expanding gas fronts having different temperatures and densities. The collision causes the gaseous mixture to become unstable, resulting in the fragmentation and condensation of the gas into large droplets, which we see as the cometary heads.

NGC 2403

Constellation: Camelopardalis. Distance: 10.4 million light years.

Right Ascension: 07 hours : 36.9 minutes
Declination: +65 degrees : 36 minutes

The luminous spiral galaxy NGC 2403 bears a high rate of star formation and exceptionally bright HII regions, comparable to the giant HII regions in our Local Group. A recent survey of NGC 2403 identified at least six of these monster clouds. The most luminous extended across 2,000 light years, the size of almost fifty Orion Nebulae! These giant HII regions are powered by large OB associations and often contain dozens of Wolf-Rayet candidate stars, soon to become supernovae.

M46

Also cataloged as NGC 2437. Constellation: Puppis. Distance: 5,400 light years.

Right Ascension: 07 hours : 41.8 minutes
Declination: -14 degrees : 49 minutes

Although a rich cluster in its own right, M46 is better known for its guest, the planetary nebula NGC 2438. Spanning 30 light years, M46 is one of only four clusters identified with planetary nebulae. The planetary nebula is not believed to be related to any members of the cluster but rather superimposed or possibly passing through M46. This assumption is based on several factors. First, the cluster and planetary nebula move at different velocities. Second, the planetary nebula represents a late evolutionary phase. This requires at least one billion years to achieve for low- and intermediate-mass stars, far exceeding the age of M46, thought to be a considerably evolved middle-aged cluster about 300 million years old.

M44

PRAESEPE

Also cataloged as NGC 2632 and popularly known as the Beehive Cluster.
Constellation: Cancer. Distance: 577 light years.

Right Ascension: 08 hours : 40.1 minutes
Declination: +19 degrees : 59 minutes

The open cluster known as Praesepe, Latin for "manger," is one of the earliest celestial objects known to man. Many cultures have recorded observations of it since ancient times. Galileo was the first to turn a telescope on Praesepe and to note that many stars composed the "small cloud." The cluster spans about 10 light years and includes approximately 200 to 350 members confirmed by common motion. It is an older cluster, formed some 730 million years ago.

M67

Also cataloged as NGC 2682. Constellation: Cancer. Distance: 2,600 light years.

Right Ascension: 08 hours : 50.4 minutes
Declination: +11 degrees : 49 minutes

Unlike most open clusters, M67 is truly ancient. Its roughly five hundred members are estimated at four billion years old, almost as old as our solar system. It is unclear how some clusters manage to survive for so long while most disperse after several hundred million years. Observations have found two basic populations of open clusters: a dominant population with a mean age of about 200 million years and a much older subset with an age of about four billion years. The older populations appear to be located in the outer disk of the galaxy and often farther from the disk plane, where molecular clouds tend to be sparser. One theory postulates that these unusual orbits isolate the clusters from the typical interactions, such as collisions with molecular clouds, that often shred galactic clusters. M67 is perched some 1,400 light years above the galactic plane.

NGC 2841

Constellation: Ursa Major. Distance: 46 million light years.

Right Ascension: 09 hours : 22.0 minutes
Declination: +50 degrees : 58 minutes

The compact spiral galaxy NGC 2841 belongs to the class of galaxies known as flocculent spirals because they have short, patchy spiral arms that are fragmented and loosely organized. Among other celestial phenomenon, the galaxy has hosted four supernovae in the last century. NGC 2841 has what is known as a decoupled nucleus, meaning the chemical abundances of the nucleus are substantially different from its inner bulge. The decoupled nucleus most likely has an external origin, such as an encounter with a gas-rich galaxy several billion years ago. Gas was accreted from the smaller galaxy and settled into the nucleus, where it established an independent rotation.

N
E

NGC 2903

Constellation: Leo. Distance: 25 million light years.

Right Ascension: 09 hours : 32.2 minutes
Declination: +21 degrees : 30 minutes

Similar to other barred spirals, NGC 2903 possesses a prominent nuclear star-forming ring, placing it in the class of hot-spot galaxies. These luminous galaxies produce high rates of star formation but fall short of the prototypical starburst galaxies. NGC 2903 also has several supergiant HII regions, similar in luminosity to 30 Doradus in the Large Magellanic Cloud.

A significant percentage of barred galaxies show a nuclear star-forming ring in the central 3,000 light years of the galaxy. Computer simulations show that bars may provide an efficient mechanism for transporting gas and other disk components into the central regions of galaxies, triggering starbursts.

M81

BODE'S GALAXY

Also cataloged as NGC 3031. Constellation: Ursa Major. Distance: 12 million light years.

Right Ascension: 09 hours : 55.6 minutes
Declination: +69 degrees: 04 minutes

The German astronomer Johann Elert Bode discovered in 1774 the grand design galaxy that still carries his name. Bode's Galaxy is the brightest member of the nearby galactic group called the M81 Group. This group contains at least twenty-five other members, including the peculiar galaxies M82 and NGC 3077, and many dwarf galaxies. The core galaxies of the group all interact and are embedded in a large, extended gas cloud. Several of the dwarf galaxies likely formed recently from condensing tidal debris pulled from the dominant members during major encounters.

M82

CIGAR GALAXY

Also cataloged as NGC 3034. Constellation: Ursa Major. Distance: 12 million light years.

Right Ascension: 09 hours : 55.8 minutes
Declination: +69 degrees : 41 minutes

The prototypical irregular starburst galaxy known as the Cigar Galaxy forms a well-known pair with Bode's Galaxy. The closest starburst galaxy to the Milky Way, the Cigar Galaxy shows a rate of star formation ten times greater than our galaxy. A violent gravitational interaction between M81 and M82 is believed to have triggered the starburst activity 300 million to 600 million years ago.

A starburst epoch may last for ten million years or more. During this period, stars can form at rates up to hundreds of times greater than those observed in normal galaxies. The accumulated brightness of new massive stars makes these galaxies some of the most luminous. The wave of star formation can sweep through the galaxy's entire central region, consuming vast amounts of gas. When the gas clouds are depleted, star formation eventually ceases.

The bursts of star formation have produced dramatic effects on the Cigar Galaxy. Stellar winds from thousands of new stars and supernova-driven shock fronts have ejected ultrahot gases extending from the galactic core several thousand light years. The superheated gases are collectively known as a galactic superwind.

Whirlpool Galaxy

SPRING

The Realm of the Galaxies

Yeah, I know nobody knows
where it comes and where it goes.

—Aerosmith, "Dream On"

Although galaxies can be observed year-round, springtime is truly the season of the galaxy. As winter becomes spring, and the great nebulae fade from view, a treat is in store for those who favor the truly distant worlds: the galaxies. The essence of springtime is the myriad galactic treasures of the truly deep and distant sky. Within the grasp of a moderate-sized telescope lie countless distant worlds, each with its own distinct form. From graceful and majestic spirals to giant cannibalizing ellipticals, to self-destructing irregular types, the constellations of Virgo, Coma Berenices, Ursa Major, and Canes Venatici hold a glorious assortment of galactic specimens, enough to occupy an observer or astrophotographer for several lifetimes.

Since Hubble's seminal work establishing galaxies as separate "island universes," astronomers know that galaxies are not isolated but actually interact with one another on a vast cosmic scale. Galaxies exist not only in clusters but also within vast large-scale structures known as superclusters. From our standpoint in the Milky Way, the closest giant agglomeration of galaxies is the Virgo cluster, which contains well over 2,500 galaxies. The Virgo cluster together with our Local Group constitutes the Virgo Supercluster.

Galaxies are truly ancient structures and how they evolved is a source of intense research and debate among astronomers. What they look like today is the outcome of events occurring over eons since the Big Bang. The prevailing view is that the large, mature, stable galaxies of today formed from the hierarchal accretion of smaller systems, meaning an earlier epoch of intense cannibalization of smaller galaxies have contributed to the final stable form of all spiral galaxies we see today, including our Milky Way.

Facing North

CASSIOPEIA
PERSEUS
Facing NE
Facing NW
CEPHEUS
Capella
Polaris α
URSA MINOR
AURIGA
CYGNUS
DRACO
Little Dipper
β
Deneb
LYNX
GEMINI
Vega
LYRA
Castor
Pollux
Albireo
α
Big Dipper
Mizar & Alcor
α
β
HERCULES
η
ζ
δ
γ
URSA MAJOR
CANCER
CANIS MINOR
α
Procyon
CORONA BOREALIS
Zenith
α CANES VENATICI
LEO MINOR
α
Facing West
Facing East
α
BOÖTES
Sickle
Regulus
α
COMA BERENICES
LEO
α
Denebola
β
Arcturus
SERPENS (CAPUT)
α
EQUATOR
SEXTANS
Alphard
α
HYDRA
OPHIUCHUS
VIRGO
γ
τ
ε
β
CRATER
α
Spica
CORVUS
α
ECLIPTIC
Antares
SCORPIUS
LIBRA
α
CRATER
α
Facing SW
Facing SE
CENTAURUS

Facing South

Star magnitudes
−1 0 1 2 3 4

Variable star   Double star

When To Use This Star Map
Early March: 2 a.m.
Late March: 1 a.m.
Early April: midnight
Late April: 11 p.m.
Early May: 10 p.m.
Late May: Dusk

These are standard times. If daylight-saving time is in effect, add one hour. Use the chart within an hou
or so of the times listed. Hold the chart in front of you and turn it so the yellow label for the directio
you're facing is at the bottom, right-side up. The stars above the chart's horizon should match those i
the sky. This chart is valid for observers between approximately 30° and 50° north latitude.

NGC 3079 and Q0957+561

Constellation: Ursa Major. Distance to NGC 3079: 50 million light years. Distance to Q0957+561: 9.1 billion light years.

Right Ascension: 10 hours : 02.0 minutes
Declination: +55 degrees: 41 minutes

A remarkable type of active galaxy is the quasar (quasi-stellar radio source), which appears as a starlike point source but is located at an enormous distance. Most astronomers believe they represent very distant galaxies with extremely active nuclei. Their light output is enormous, making them the most luminous objects in the universe.

NGC 3079 is a significant and worthy galaxy in its own right, but the highlight of the accompanying photograph is the unassuming presence of the first gravitationally lensed quasar ever discovered, Q0957+561. The paired stellar objects appear to blend imperceptibly into the foreground star field. The true nature of the pair first became apparent in 1979 when their remarkable red shifts (a measure of their recessional velocity that translates to distance) were discovered, implying two incredibly luminous objects at remote extragalactic distances. Further studies showed that the pair indeed represents a single active galaxy whose double image is a mirage.

Q0957+561 is an extremely remote object whose light was emitted over nine billion years ago, when the universe was a fraction of its present age. The optical illusion of the multiple images is created by the presence of a massive foreground structure, in this case a giant elliptical galaxy, referred to as the lens. The lens distorts the fabric of space, causing the light from the more distant quasar to bend around it. Because bending is not symmetric, observers will see multiple images of the same object.

Q0957+561

E
↑
└→Z

Hickson 44

Individual galaxies cataloged as NGC 3190, NGC 3193, NGC 3185, and NGC 3187.
Constellation: Leo. Distance: 60 million light years.

Right Ascension: 10 hours : 18.1 minutes
Declination: +21 degrees : 50 minutes

In 1982, the Canadian astronomer Paul Hickson, using the red prints from the Palomar Observatory Sky Survey, published a catalog of 462 galaxies thought to exist in compact groupings. These groupings are now referred to as Hickson Compact Groups. Compact groups typically comprise four or five galaxies in close proximity to one another. They are among the densest concentrations of galaxies known, comparable to the centers of rich galaxy clusters. Compact groups are worthy of intense study, as they provide a rich opportunity to study galaxy interactions and merger events.

Current theory postulates that compact groups represent physically related galaxies in the process of merging into a single object, likely an elliptical galaxy. Hickson groups therefore offer snapshots of various stages in this merging process. The four dominant members of Hickson 44 are three spirals and an elliptical galaxy. Signs of tidal encounters are evident as NGC 3190 (above center), the dominant edge-on spiral, shows considerable warping of its dust lane on the side near to NGC 3187 (lower right). NGC 3187 also shows tidal tails above and below its disk plane.

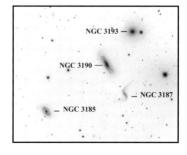

E
N

NGC 3372

ETA CARINAE NEBULA

Constellation: Carina. Distance: 7,500 light years.

Right Ascension: 10 hours : 43.8 minutes
Declination: -59 degrees : 52 minutes

A bright photogenic patch of the southern Milky Way holds one of the most enigmatic and exotic stars known. Eta Carinae is the centerpiece and ionizing star of a great HII region, the Eta Carinae Nebula. The nebula spans some 260 light years. The great star weighs in at some 100 to 150 solar masses and shines with the light output of five million suns. One of the most massive stars known, Eta Carinae pushes the theoretical limits of stellar energy output. The young supergiant pumps out as much energy in six seconds as our sun does in an entire year. Its prodigious stellar wind blows off the equivalent mass of Jupiter each year, exceeding our sun's yearly rate of mass loss a hundred billion fold.

Because of its extraordinary mass, the star is expected to end its life as a great supernova in the near future. An energy outburst of this order could possibly devastate star fields and planets within a few thousand light years radius of Eta.

M95, M96, and M105
LEO I GROUP

Also cataloged as NGC 3351, NGC 3368, and NGC 3379. Constellation: Leo. Distance: 37 million light years.

Right Ascension: 10 hours : 44.0 minutes
Declination: +11 degrees : 42 minutes

The bright spiral galaxies M95 (upper right) and M96 (left) and the elliptical galaxy M105 (leftmost galaxy in lower right photo) make up the dominant members of the Leo I Group. This sparse galactic grouping has been of great importance during the last decade in establishing a standard scale for the measurement of extragalactic distances. Evidence has shown that all three galaxies lie at the same distance. The close relationship of the two spirals along with M105, the closest elliptical galaxy to our sun, has provided an unusually clean route of determining the all-important and elusive Hubble's constant. Hubble's constant gives the rate of recession of galaxies per unit distance away. Edwin Hubble's discovery that distant galaxies are receding more rapidly than closer ones was instrumental to the development of the big bang theory. The refinement of Hubble's constant has great implications for cosmology and our knowledge about the ultimate fate of the universe.

E
↑
└→ Z

NGC 3521

Constellation: Leo. Distance: 35 million light years.

Right Ascension: 11 hours : 05.8 minutes
Declination: -00 degrees : 02 minutes

NGC 3521 bears a prominent flocculent design. About one-third of all spiral galaxies have a flocculent structure to some degree. The other two-thirds have the classic grand-design structure with two symmetric prominent spiral arms. For unknown reasons, flocculent galaxies often show a prominent halo. The optical counterpart of NGC 3521's extensive gaseous halo can be seen shining well above its galactic plane.

NGC 3603 and NGC 3576

Constellation: Carina. Distance to NGC 3603: 23,000 light years. Distance to NGC 3576: 10,000 light years.

Right Ascension: 11 hours : 11.8 minutes
Declination: -61 degrees : 23 minutes

NGC 3603 (left) and NGC 3576 (right) are two of the most luminous HII regions in our galaxy, but their juxtaposition represents an illusion. Although appearing side by side, the two objects are physically unrelated. NGC 3603 is twice as distant as NGC 3576. NGC 3576 resides in the Milky Way's Sagittarius arm, while NGC 3603 is located in our galaxy's more distant Carina arm. There are some similarities, however, as both are undergoing a high rate of sequential star formation.

NGC 3603 is an extraordinary object. It is likely the most massive visible giant HII region in our galaxy, extending at least a thousand light years across and containing the mass of ten thousand suns. At its center is an extremely compact and bright cluster of massive stars. This compact grouping produces an extraordinary ionizing flux estimated to be a hundred times greater than the ultraviolet energy produced by the Orion Nebula's Trapezium cluster.

M97

Owl Nebula

Also cataloged as NGC 3587. Constellation: Ursa Major. Distance: 2,000 light years.

Right Ascension: 11 hours : 14.8 minutes
Declination: +55 degrees : 01 minutes

The Owl Nebula, an older planetary nebula, has a circular morphology and a bland inner structure. The nebula's outer halo formed from material ejected thousands of years earlier during the dying star's red-giant phase. It continues to interact with the surrounding interstellar medium as the planetary nebula moves through space. The central star is a hot dead cinder of about 0.6 solar masses, which still produces abundant radiation because of its 110,000-degree Kelvin surface temperature.

NGC 3628, M65, and M66

LEO TRIPLET

M65 also cataloged as NGC 3623. M66 also cataloged as NGC 3627.
Constellation: Leo. Distance: 30 million light years

Right Ascension: 11 hours : 18.9 minutes
Declination: +13 degrees : 05 minutes

The Leo Triplet is a well-known, conspicuous grouping of galaxies in the constellation Leo. In the photo opposite, NGC 3628 is in the upper left, M66 in the lower left, and M65 in the lower right. A close-up of NGC 3628 is below. The three galaxies all reside within one degree of one another in the sky and are thought to be physically bound as all three are the same distance from Earth. The Leo Triplet has likely been a dynamically bound interacting system for some time. Simulations suggest that these galaxies came within 80,000 light years of one another some 800 million years ago. The telltale signs of the interaction are found in subtle structural features of each galaxy.

NGC 3718

Also cataloged as Arp 214. Constellation: Ursa Major. Distance: 42.4 million light years.

Right Ascension: 11 hours : 32.6 minutes
Declination: +53 degrees : 04 minutes

The peculiar galaxy NGC 3718 (right) bears an extraordinary dust lane and a strongly warped disk, which together produce its distinctive S-shaped appearance. The dust lane runs through the galaxy's entire stellar bulge, stretching some 80,000 light years from end to end. The disk appears almost edge-on at the center and is strongly warped to almost 90 degrees—a degree of warping unheard of even among peculiar galaxies.

Using film images taken by the Palomar 200-inch telescope, American astronomer Halton Arp cataloged 338 peculiar galaxies in his 1966 *Atlas of Peculiar Galaxies*. Warping occurs relatively frequently among such irregular galaxies, although the cause is uncertain. In the case of NGC 3718, the most reasonable explanation is its close proximity to the galaxy NGC 3729 (left), which presumably exerts strong tidal forces on its neighbor's disk. The two galaxies, both members of the Ursa Major galaxy cluster, appear to orbit each other at a projected separation of 147,000 light years.

A grouping of five background galaxies 300 million light years distant, designated Arp 322, are projected to the south of NGC 3718.

M109

Also cataloged as NGC 3992. Constellation: Ursa Major. Distance: 55 million light years.

Right Ascension: 11 hours : 57.6 minutes
Declination: +53 degrees : 23 minutes

M109 is an exquisite example of a symmetric barred spiral galaxy. Its strong stellar bar component has a rounded central bulge and is surrounded by an incomplete ring from which the two tightly wound spiral arms originate. The galaxy displays an unusual absence of bright HII regions, and although knots of star-forming regions exist in the outer spiral arms, star formation is absent from the galaxy's inner regions.

M109 is a member of the Ursa Major Cluster of galaxies. Unlike the Virgo cluster, which appears to concentrate toward a core, the Ursa Major cluster is more dispersed. Its loose structure has left it relatively undefined compared to other clusters. It has about seventy-nine known major galactic members spread over about 3 million light years.

NGC 4038 and NGC 4039

ANTENNAE

Constellation: Corvus. Distance: 45 million light years.

Right Ascension: 12 hours : 01.9 minutes
Declination: -18 degrees : 52 minutes

No single event in the universe is as impressive as the collision of galaxies. Galactic interactions and mergers play a critical role in galactic evolution. Considering the immense vastness of space, collisions of these cosmic giants occur more often than one might think. Due to their enormous size, the average distance between galaxies is only twenty times greater than their diameter. The statistical outcome indicates that collisions will occur at least a few times in the life of an average galaxy. Collisions are characterized as "major" when two equal-mass galaxies collide and "minor" when a larger galaxy absorbs an object of lesser mass, such as a dwarf galaxy. Galactic collisions may take hundreds of millions, or even billions, of years to complete.

The galaxies NGC 4038 and 4039, popularly referred to as the Antennae, are the prototypical model of merging galactic systems. The galactic interaction began between 300 and 450 million years ago and will likely end in the full merger of the two behemoths some 300 million years from now.

E

Z

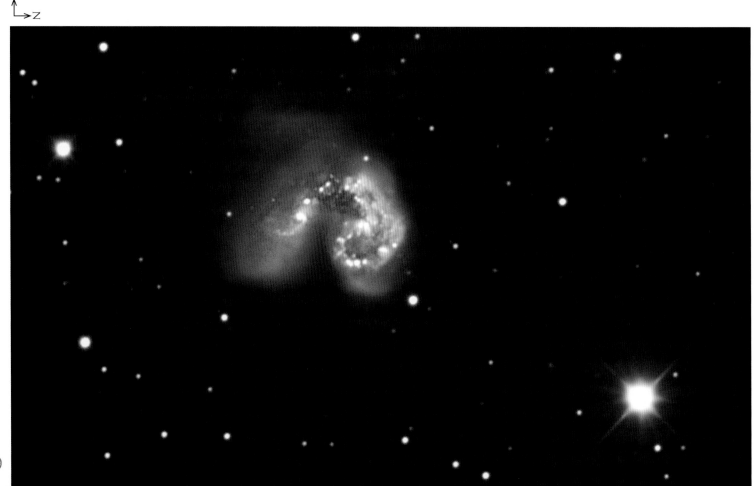

E
↑
└→ Z

M106

Also cataloged as NGC 4258. Constellation: Canes Venatici. Distance: 24 million light years.

Right Ascension: 12 hours : 19.0 minutes
Declination: +47 degrees : 18 minutes

The Seyfert galaxy M106 holds the distinction of harboring the nearest extragalactic astrophysical jet (red plume left of center). Its proximity and 72-degree incline expose the galaxy's central barred core to earthbound telescopes, giving astronomers the opportunity to learn about jet phenomenon in great detail. Jets are beams of matter and energy often arising in the cores of active galaxies. They are best observed at radio wavelengths and usually come in pairs aimed in opposite directions. Like other Seyfert galaxies, M106 shows evidence of a massive black hole (about 36 million solar masses) deep within its nucleus.

M61

Also cataloged as NGC 4303. Constellation: Virgo. Distance: 51.5 million light years.

Right Ascension: 12 hours : 21.9 minutes
Declination: +04 degrees : 28 minutes

M61 is a grand design spiral and one of the brightest and most intensively studied barred galaxies in the Virgo cluster, located along the outer edge of the cluster. Star formation occurs at a high level in M61, indicated by the numerous HII regions and high number of supernovae (four) observed in the last century. Star formation in M61 is particularly concentrated near the tips of the central bar. Central bars are known to trigger the formation of starburst rings by causing inflows of gas from the disk to the more central regions of the galaxy.

VIRGO CLUSTER

Constellation: Virgo. Distance: 60 million light years.

Right Ascension: 12 hours : 26.2 minutes
Declination: +12 degrees : 57 minutes

More than 2,500 individual galaxies reside in the Virgo Cluster of Galaxies, our Local Group's closest neighbor. Together, the two make up the Virgo Supercluster. The supercluster exerts a powerful gravitational force, drawing its members toward a central point near the mammoth elliptical galaxy M87. The Local Group has experienced the cluster's tug in the form of a general slowing of its expansion velocity over millions of years.

Many giant elliptical galaxies exist at the center of the Virgo Cluster, supporting the contention that elliptical types represent the culmination of intergalactic collisions and mergers. The Virgo galaxies have also played a key role in establishing Hubble's constant, which defines the expansion rate of the universe. Refining Hubble's constant will ultimately allow astronomers to narrow down the true age of the universe. To calculate Hubble's constant, astronomers require two values: the recessional speed of a galaxy and the precise distance to that galaxy. Establishing precise distances to remote galaxies remains one of the primary goals of modern cosmology.

NGC 4449

Constellation: Canes Venatici. Distance: 12 million light years.

Right Ascension: 12 hours : 28.2 minutes
Declination: +44 degrees : 06 minutes

Although spiral galaxies seem to get all the attention, irregular galaxies are probably the most frequently encountered type among star-forming galaxies and make up one-third to one-half of all galaxies. Hubble originally defined irregular types as having a chaotic, nonsymmetrical light distribution without spiral structure, although some irregulars do display rudimentary spiral arms. Irregulars are usually smaller, less massive, and dimmer than the giant spirals and elliptical types.

The dwarf irregular galaxy NGC 4449 features giant shells of hot gas, as well as superluminous supernova remnants, all signs of recent massive star formation. The galaxy's structure and chaotic star-forming conditions suggest a large-scale merger in its remote past.

M87

Also cataloged as NGC 4486. Constellation: Virgo. Distance: 52 million light years.

Right Ascension: 12 hours : 30.8 minutes
Declination: +12 degrees : 24 minutes

The massive galaxy M87 dominates the Virgo cluster. This powerful elliptical galaxy contains over one trillion stars, enormous by all galactic standards, and has a remarkable diameter of over a half million light years. Thousands of globular clusters, visible as fuzzy dots, mark its perimeter. Lying at the center of the Virgo cluster, M87 produces much of the cluster's energy output in the form of X-ray and radio-wave emission. The giant galaxy possesses a famous unidirectional jet, 6,500 light years long, arising from its nucleus.

Many galaxies with active galactic nuclei show jet phenomenon. However, no other jet observed even remotely matches the brightness of M87's jet (above). Arising from a rotating disk of stars and matter known as an accretion disk, the jet gives up mass to what astronomers believe is the most massive black hole known in the universe so far. This black hole packs a mass of three billion suns into an area the size of our solar system. As material from the accretion disk falls into the black hole, mass is converted to energy through a process even more efficient than nuclear fusion. The jet forms as heated gases are pulled away and propelled from the black hole along the axis of rotation. Light and radio emissions arise from high-energy electrons that spiral around the jet's intense magnetic field.

NGC 4565

NEEDLE GALAXY

Constellation: Coma Berenices. Distance: 32.6 million light years.

Right Ascension: 12 hours : 36.3 minutes
Declination: +25 degrees : 59 minutes

The Needle Galaxy's symmetry and grace have elevated it to an iconic status among galaxies. At an inclination of 86 degrees, the impressive edge-on disk is one of the largest and most massive of the relatively nearby spiral galaxies. The Needle Galaxy's size (more than 100,000 light years), mass (200 billion suns), number of globular clusters (200), and its rotational velocity all bear remarkable similarities to the Milky Way. A peculiar feature is the warping of its outer disk edges. Warping occurs in about 50 percent of all spirals, including the Milky Way. The warping of the Needle Galaxy's disk is believed to be due to an encounter with its companion NGC 4562 some 300 million years ago.

M58

Also cataloged as NGC 4579. Constellation: Virgo. Distance: 65 million light years.

Right Ascension: 12 hours : 37.7 minutes
Declination: +11 degrees : 49 minutes

The bright, strongly barred galaxy M58 is one of the most gas-poor galaxies known, likely due to its proximity to M87 near the center of the rich Virgo cluster. Galaxies located deep in crowded clusters often display profound deficiencies in their neutral gas content. Several factors explain the gas loss, including tidal stripping by galaxy-galaxy interactions and a phenomenon known as ram pressure, where a galaxy moving through the dense intergalactic gas of a rich cluster has much of its interstellar gas stripped from it.

N
E

M104

SOMBRERO GALAXY

Also cataloged as NGC 4594. Constellation: Virgo. Distance: 31 million light years.

Right Ascension: 12 hours : 40.0 minutes
Declination: -11 degrees : 37 minutes

The Sombrero Galaxy makes a truly remarkable sight with its prominent glowing bulge transected by a thick, pronounced spiral disk. This luminous galaxy has the mass of 800 billion suns. Its edge-on orientation has provided astronomers with insights into the organization of matter in spiral galaxies.

The Sombrero Galaxy has a rich population of globular clusters with several of the more impressive ones easily visible in the photograph. By some estimates, it contains 1,100 globular clusters, far more than the 150 or so in the Milky Way. The Sombrero Galaxy is on a growing list of galaxies known to possess a supermassive black hole in its nucleus. Its black hole contains a monstrous one billion solar masses.

N
E

NGC 4631

WHALE GALAXY

Constellation: Canes Venatici. Distance: 25 million light years.

Right Ascension: 12 hours : 42.1 minutes
Declination: +32 degrees : 32 minutes

NGC 4631 is a considerably disturbed edge-on starburst galaxy, similar in many respects to the Cigar and Sculptor galaxies. It offers a diverse range of unusual features, many of which have resulted from galactic interactions. The galaxy is undergoing complex tidal interactions with two of its close neighbors: NGC 4627 (above center), a dwarf elliptical type, and NGC 4656, an edge-on spiral (not in the image). Large tidal spurs of molecular gas reach out from NGC 4631 to its companion galaxies, confirming the physical relationship. Optical images reveal the counterpart of these tidal spurs in the form of a faint light bridge to NGC 4627.

E
N

M94

Also cataloged as NGC 4736. Constellation: Canes Venatici. Distance: 15 million light years.

Right Ascension: 12 hours : 50.9 minutes
Declination: +41 degrees : 07 minutes

The close starburst galaxy M94 comprises a series of ringlike structures. It possesses one of the highest optical-surface-brightness nuclei known. Its center contains a stellar bar 1,400 light years across. At a radius of about 3,500 light years lies an almost perfectly circular starburst ring. The bright ring hosts prominent HII regions, young supernova remnants, and bright young stars formed during the latest starburst epoch, which began some ten million years ago. The starburst ring is surrounded by a massive oval-shaped disk of older yellowish stars and an outer ring of very faint disk material, which exists some 18,000 light years from the center.

A nuclear bar creates a powerful torque on the disk components, which in turn alters the galactic internal dynamics of mass distribution. A redistribution of matter occurs, forming structures called resonance rings. Gas inflows from elsewhere in the disk tend to concentrate in the rings, triggering star formation.

E
↑
└→Z

NGC 4725

Constellation: Coma Berenices. Distance: 41 million light years.

Right Ascension: 12 hours : 50.4 minutes
Declination: +25 degrees : 30 minutes

A ringlike zone of HII regions and active star formation places NGC 4725 in a distinct morphological subgroup known as ringed galaxies. This ring is believed to occur when a bar alters a galaxy's internal dynamics, resulting in a phenomenon called "orbital resonances," which in turn leads to the ringlike structures. The presence of a central bar along the long axis of NGC 4725's inner ring supports this explanation. The rings almost always support zones of heightened star formation.

M64

BLACK EYE GALAXY

Also cataloged as NGC 4826. Constellation: Coma Berenices. Distance: 24.5 million light years.

Right Ascension: 12 hours : 56.7 minutes
Declination: +21 degrees : 41 minutes

A prominent dust lane complex runs asymmetrically across the northeastern side of the nearby and relatively isolated spiral galaxy M64. This peculiar structure has given the galaxy its popular moniker the Black Eye Galaxy. The dusty environs of its central region, dubbed the "Evil Eye," emit light through the photoluminescence of nanometer-sized dust particles. Star-forming regions in this central region produce ultraviolet radiation, which interacts with the abundant dust. This phenomenon may explain the brightness of the conspicuous dust lane complex.

NGC 4945

Constellation: Centaurus. 13 million light years.

Right Ascension: 13 hours : 05.4 minutes
Declination: -49 degrees : 28 minutes

Thick dust obscures the physical appearance of the nearby edge-on galaxy NGC 4945. The galaxy belongs to the Centaurus group, which contains another famous galaxy, NGC 5128. NGC 4945 is remarkable in that it is both a starburst and a Seyfert galaxy. In fact, it has one of the most heavily obscured Seyfert nuclei known. Dust and gas heavily attenuate the visible light of the starburst; however, its presence is revealed at infrared wavelengths.

E
↑
└→Z

NGC 5033

Constellation: Canes Venatici. Distance: 43 million light years.

Right Ascension: 13 hours : 13.4 minutes
Declination: +36 degrees : 36 minutes

The massive galaxy NGC 5033 bears a pronounced spiral structure and nuclear bulge. A peculiar feature of NGC 5033 is the presence of two distinct nuclei. The optical nucleus is located in the true dynamic center of the galaxy; however, a Seyfert-type nucleus is displaced from the optical nucleus by about 3 arcseconds. A number of galaxies, including the Andromeda Galaxy, possess an active nucleus located off-center from the true dynamic center. In most cases, astronomers believe that a large-scale galactic merger produced the separate nuclei. The Seyfert nucleus of NGC 5033 likely represents the captured nucleus of a less dominant galaxy.

M63

SUNFLOWER GALAXY

Also cataloged as NGC 5055. Constellation: Canes Venatici. Distance: 23.4 million light years.

Right Ascension: 13 hours : 15.8 minutes
Declination: +42 degrees : 02 minutes

Whereas grand design galaxies have well-defined spiral arms, the Sunflower Galaxy lacks a well-defined spiral structure. Its fragmented and patchy arms place it in the class of flocculent spiral galaxies. Since flocculent galaxies apparently lack the density waves believed to create spiral arms and in turn star formation, how does star formation occur? One hypothesis proposed by astronomers Philip E. Seiden and Humberto Gerola in 1982 is the stochastic model, which suggests that self-propagating star formation in random areas of the disk can occur in some galaxies without the influence of density waves. Computer simulations support this model. In fact, self-propagating star formation occurs commonly on a smaller scale in the spiral arms of grand design galaxies.

NGC 5128

CENTAURUS A

Constellation: Centaurus. Distance: 12.5 million light years.

Right Ascension: 13 hours : 25.5 minutes
Declination: -43 degrees : 01 minutes

NGC 5128 is the prototypical postmerger galaxy. Several prominent features suggest a large-scale merger about a billion years ago: its large elliptical structure, which is responsible for about 90 percent of its luminosity, and its massive central disk of stars, dust, and gas. Tidal streams of young stars have also been identified in the complex shell structure of its halo, thought to have occurred some 300 million years ago, when NGC 5128 cannibalized a nearby gas-rich dwarf galaxy.

In 1949, NGC 5128 was found to be a loud source of radio energy, in fact the loudest radio source in its region of the sky. As a radio galaxy, it releases one thousand times the radio energy of the Milky Way in the form of large bidirectional radio lobes that extend some 800,000 light years. The source of the radio emission is very compact, about 10 light days across, and is believed to represent a supermassive black hole in the galaxy's center with a total mass of between 200 million to 1 billion suns.

NGC 5139

OMEGA CENTAURI

Constellation: Centaurus. Distance: 15,000 light years.

Right Ascension: 13 hours : 26.8 minutes
Declination: -47 degrees : 29 minutes

Omega Centauri represents the most massive and brightest of all known globular clusters in the Milky Way. Its ten million stars place it on the size scale of a small galaxy. Its age qualifies it as one of the most ancient objects in the universe. Aside from its impressive size and brilliance, Omega has attracted attention for the diversity of its stellar populations. Different populations of stars likely occurred by mergers and captures of stellar populations over the cluster's long history.

M51

WHIRLPOOL GALAXY

Also cataloged as NGC 5194. Constellation: Canes Venatici. Distance: 37 million light years.

Right Ascension: 13 hours : 29.9 minutes
Declination: +47 degrees : 12 minutes

The Whirlpool Galaxy was the first spiral structure ever observed (1850) at a time when the true nature of galaxies was unknown. Its graceful spiral form has granted it iconic status and established it as an accepted showpiece of the night sky. The Whirlpool Galaxy also dramatically demonstrates an interacting pair of galaxies. Simulations suggest that NGC 5195, the irregular companion, is located well behind the Whirlpool Galaxy and that the two galaxies are now traveling away from each other. Some 70 million years ago, the less massive NGC 5195 encountered the disk of the Whirlpool Galaxy in a highly inclined passage. The ultimate fate of the complex will likely be a final merger in about one billion to two billion years.

M83
SOUTHERN PINWHEEL

Also cataloged as NGC 5236. Constellation: Hydra. Distance: 14.7 million light years.

Right Ascension: 13 hours : 37.0 minutes
Declination: -29 degrees : 52 minutes

The Southern Pinwheel is a nearby face-on barred spiral with a classic grand design form. The galaxy prolifically produces supernovae, including six observed in the past century, second only to NGC 6946, which has produced a record eight supernovae. The high number of supernovae indicates an exceptionally high rate of star formation, justifying its classification as a starburst galaxy, similar to other well-known starburst galaxies, such as the Cigar and Sculptor galaxies.

M3

Also cataloged as NGC 5272. Constellation: Canes Venatici. Distance: 33,900 light years.

Right Ascension: 13 hours : 42.2 minutes
Declination: +28 degrees : 23 minutes

A superb visual and photographic object, the globular cluster M3 contains about a half million stars and lies at a distance of 33,900 light years. M3 possesses one of the densest core regions for a globular cluster, having 50 percent of its total mass within the central 22 light years. One of the most studied clusters in the galaxy, M3 is particularly known for its unusual number of variable stars, especially the subtype RR Lyrae variables. These important stars are short-period pulsating variables having a period from 0.2 to 2 days. Like Cepheid variables, they exhibit a close relationship between the period and the luminosity, making them reliable distance indicators. Although not quite as massive or luminous as Cepheids, they are useful for measuring distances to clusters in the Milky Way.

M101

PINWHEEL GALAXY

Also cataloged as NGC 5457. Constellation: Ursa Major. Distance: 23.5 million light years.

Right Ascension: 14 hours : 03.2 minutes
Declination: +54 degrees : 21 minutes

One of the final entries in Charles Messier's list of comet imposters was M101, popularly known as the Pinwheel Galaxy. The dominant member of a small group of nine galaxies, the Pinwheel is truly a giant. With a visible diameter of 170,000 light years, it is one of the largest disk galaxies known. Although its size exceeds that of our Milky Way, its overall mass is similar. A high number of giant HII regions populate the Pinwheel Galaxy's spiral arms. Star clusters with an enormous ionization flux power the extraordinary luminosity of these nebulae. An exceptionally high concentration of massive stars places some of these clusters in the category of super star clusters, which typically possess a cumulative stellar mass of 100,000 to 1,000,000 suns.

M5

Also cataloged as NGC 5904. Constellation: Serpens. Distance: 24,500 light years.

Right Ascension: 15 hours : 18.6 minutes
Declination: +02 degrees : 05 minutes

M5 is one of the oldest globular clusters, at an estimated age of 13 billion years. It shows an intermediate level of metallicity, a term referring to elements heavier than helium. These heavier elements were not present when the universe formed and could only be created through nucleosynthesis in star cores. Although globular clusters as a group are largely metal-deficient, they are divided into two groupings of low metallicity. Astronomers measure metallicity by analyzing the spectra of a star and computing the iron to hydrogen ratio. Metallicity seems to decrease as the distance from the galactic center increases, suggesting a possible separate origin or even a captured origin of metal-poor globular clusters from a dwarf satellite galaxy in the remote past.

Summer Milky Way

SUMMER

The Milky Way: Coming Home

The nights of wonder
With friends surrounded . . .
The endless river
Forever and ever

—David Gilmour/Polly Samson

From a dark place on a clear summer night, a spectacle unfolds that transcends time and connects us back to countless generations of humanity. The grandeur of our home galaxy as witnessed from our small planet is a singular experience every human being should have. The summer Milky Way as seen by the naked eye comprises several vast and overlapping spiral arms and the combined light of hundreds of millions of stars. Sadly, this experience has eluded many people in modern times with the growing light of civilization. Before the modern era, humans gazed at the star clouds of the Milky Way and wondered about their meaning. Today, we know the nature of those milky star clouds but the experience is no less inspiring.

Our own galaxy may very well hold the secret to the forces that drive billions of other spiral galaxies. Of supreme interest to astronomers is what lurks at the true center of the Milky Way. Our sun is only 26,000 light years from the center of the galaxy, offering a bird's-eye view of this tantalizing region. Immense dust hides our galactic center at optical wavelengths; fortunately, astronomers can use radio, infrared, and X-ray wavelengths to peer through this dust.

The true galactic center harbors an enigmatic object known as Sagittarius A, long known to be one of the most powerful radio sources in the sky, second only to the sun. Radio and X-ray observations have revealed that within the 30 light years surrounding Sagittarius A, things really start to get strange. This is an extremely compact region containing many millions of stars. Close to the center are a number of young blue supergiant stars among older red giants and scattered supernova remnants. Astronomers postulate that multiple epochs of star formation have occurred here, spawned by collisions of closely compacted molecular clouds. Several stars within a few light years of Sagittarius A show orbital velocities so rapid that the only explanation is a central object of extremely concentrated mass. The incredibly massive object occupies a space of only 0.1 astronomical units (about 1 light minute) but contains at least 2.6 million solar masses. Sagittarius A must be so compact and massive that it can only be explained by a supermassive black hole at the extreme center of our galaxy. Astronomers now assume that supermassive black holes exist at the center of most, if not all, spiral galaxies.

SUMMER NIGHT SKY

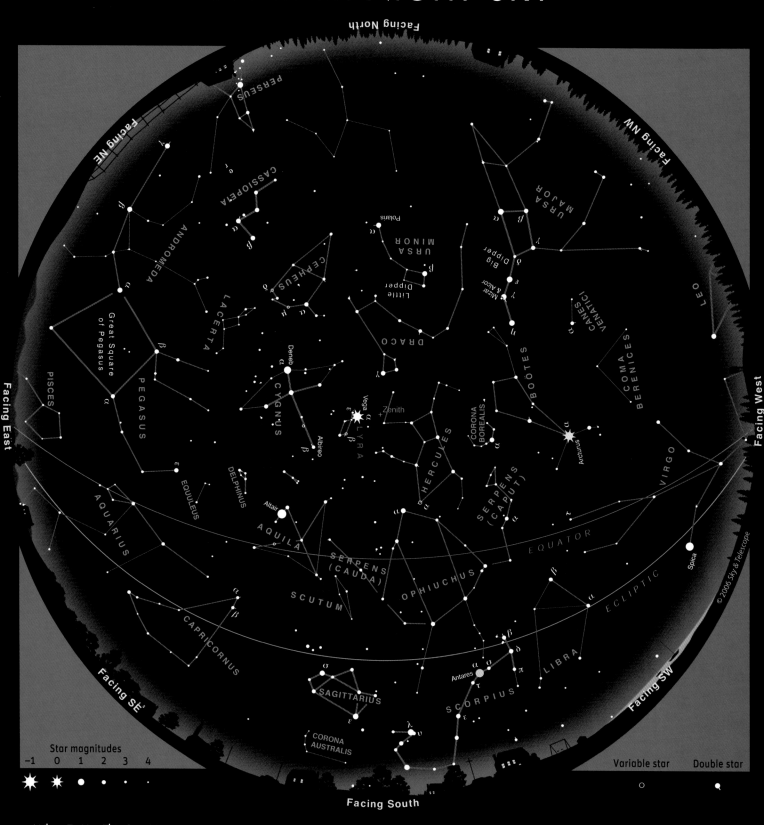

Facing North

Facing NE · Facing East · Facing SE · Facing South · Facing SW · Facing West · Facing NW

PERSEUS · CASSIOPEIA · ANDROMEDA · PEGASUS · Great Square of Pegasus · PISCES · LACERTA · CEPHEUS · URSA MINOR · Polaris · Little Dipper · DRACO · URSA MAJOR · Big Dipper · Mizar & Alcor · BOÖTES · CANES VENATICI · COMA BERENICES · LEO · CYGNUS · Deneb · Albireo · LYRA · Vega · Zenith · HERCULES · CORONA BOREALIS · Arcturus · VIRGO · EQUULEUS · DELPHINUS · AQUILA · Altair · SERPENS (CAPUT) · SERPENS (CAUDA) · SCUTUM · OPHIUCHUS · EQUATOR · Spica · AQUARIUS · CAPRICORNUS · SAGITTARIUS · CORONA AUSTRALIS · SCORPIUS · Antares · LIBRA · ECLIPTIC

© 2006 Sky & Telescope

Star magnitudes
−1 0 1 2 3 4

Variable star   Double star

When To Use This Star Map
Early June: 1 a.m.
Late June: midnight
Early July: 11 p.m.
Late July: 10 p.m.
Early August: 9 p.m.
Late August: Dusk

These are standard times. If daylight-saving time is in effect, add one hour. Use the chart within an hour or so of the times listed. Hold the chart in front of you and turn it so the yellow label for the direction you're facing is at the bottom, right-side up. The stars above the chart's horizon should match those in the sky. This chart is valid for observers between approximately 30° and 50° north latitude.

Abell 2151

HERCULES GALAXY CLUSTER

Constellation: Hercules. Distance: 500 million light years.

Right Ascension: 16 hours : 05.3 minutes
Declination: +17 degrees : 45 minutes

The Hercules Galaxy Cluster dominates the much larger collection of galaxies known as the Hercules supercluster, which spans some 6 degrees of sky. The supercluster belongs to a huge sheetlike megastructure of galaxies known as the Great Wall. The Great Wall also includes the Coma and Leo galaxy clusters and extends along a filament-shaped collection of galaxy clusters 500 million light years long, terminating at one end with the Hercules cluster. The Great Wall was the first megastructure of its kind discovered in the 1980s. The largest gravitationally bound structures known in the cosmos, superclusters can reach enormous sizes, up to several hundred million light years, and are often juxtaposed against large voids in space where few galaxies exist. Their existence indicates that galaxies are not evenly distributed in the universe but are arranged in large coherent structures of clusters, superclusters, walls, and filaments. Astronomers estimate that ten million superclusters exist in the observable universe.

E ← N

IC 4604

RHO OPHIUCHUS NEBULA

Constellation: Ophiuchus. Distance: 500 light years.

Right Ascension: 16 hours : 25.5 minutes
Declination: -23 degrees : 27 minutes

A colorful orb of nebulosity decorates the region surrounding the bright triple star Rho Ophiuchus. Probably no other region provides such an impressive spectacle of colorful glowing gases juxtaposed against riverlike channels of Milky Way dust. Rho Ophiuchi is the triple star system surrounded by the brilliant blue reflection nebula IC 4604 at the top of the image. The region is highlighted by the bright star Antares, a red supergiant forty thousand times more luminous than our sun. Antares is truly immense. With a diameter of 800 million kilometers, it is one of the few stars with a measurable disk. Antares lies embedded in an unusual yellow cloud formed by the ionization of the fierce stellar winds blown by the dying star. The bright globular cluster M4 is seen to the right of Antares.

NGC 6164 and NGC 6165

Constellation: Norma. Distance: 4,200 light years.

Right Ascension: 16 hours : 34.0 minutes
Declination: -48 degrees : 06 minutes

NGC 6164 and NGC 6165 make up a fascinating S-shaped bipolar nebula surrounding the peculiar massive star HD 148937. Although astronomers initially believed the region represented a planetary nebula, it is now understood to be a shell-like ejected nebula formed by the winds of its young central star. Windblown nebulae are usually considered the outcome of Wolf-Rayet stars, but in the case of this nebula, the central star is a young O-type supergiant of 40 solar masses. Relatively few examples of such objects are known to exist. The central star now bathes the surrounding condensations of dense gas with its fierce stellar winds. The winds are sculpting the surrounding gas into a symmetric bipolar structure.

NGC 6193 and NGC 6188

Constellation: Ara. Distance: 4,300 light years.

Right Ascension: 16 hours : 40.5 minutes
Declination: -48 degrees : 47 minutes

NGC 6193 is a remarkable young stellar cluster at the core of the Ara OB1 stellar association. The stars of this association span a full square degree of southern sky. The cluster is embedded in an area cloaked by thick gas clouds and lanes of dust. The hottest stars of the cluster, two closely spaced O-type giants (the bright stars in the photograph), provide the sole illumination source of the entire emission nebula NGC 6188. NGC 6164 (see page 129) can be seen in lower left.

M13

GREAT GLOBULAR CLUSTER IN HERCULES

Also cataloged as NGC 6205. Constellation: Hercules. Distance: 25,100 light years.

Right Ascension: 16 hours : 41.7 minutes
Declination: +36 degrees : 28 minutes

Arguably the most celebrated northern globular cluster, the Great Globular Cluster in Hercules contains several hundred thousand stars crowded into a space just 145 light years across. The cluster members are almost all highly evolved low-mass main sequence stars. Images of M13 and most globular clusters are dominated by red giants, which are typically two thousand times more luminous than our sun. To get a sense of relative luminosities, if we were to look back on our sun from M13, it would not be apparent visually using even the largest telescopes.

M7

Also cataloged as NGC 6475. Constellation: Scorpius. Distance: 780 light years.

Right Ascension: 17 hours : 53.9 minutes
Declination: -34 degrees : 49 minutes

M7 is a bright and populous cluster with its brightest blue members projected on a crowded background of dense Milky Way star fields. M7 is an important astronomical object, being the closest prototypical middle-aged cluster at an age of about 220 million years. M7 contains about a hundred stars and extends over 20 light years of space projected on 1.3 degrees of sky.

NGC 6543

CAT'S EYE NEBULA

Constellation: Draco. Distance: 3,000 light years.

Right Ascension: 17 hours : 58.6 minutes
Declination: +66 degrees : 38 minutes

The planetary nebula known as the Cat's Eye Nebula has been around for some 18,000 years. The former core of the dead star is now a compact cinder, a white dwarf emitting powerful winds and radiation that ionize the layers of the previously ejected stellar envelope. A gradient of ages defines each gaseous layer. The outermost halo (shown in the image surrounding the central planetary nebula) shines faintly, ejected some 60,000 years ago in the stellar winds of the dying star. The innermost bright layer is only 1,000 years old, while each subsequent layer is about 1,500 years older than its inner neighbor.

The Cat's Eye Nebula holds the distinction of being the first planetary nebula to have its spectrum taken. In 1864, Sir William Huggins found three bright emission lines, a blue line identified as hydrogen and two mysterious green lines never before seen. At the time, astronomers believed the mysterious lines came from an exotic new element, which they named "nebulium." It wasn't until 1926 that the origin of the green lines was identified as oxygen.

Because they do not occur naturally on Earth, the two strong emission lines are known as the "forbidden lines" of doubly ionized oxygen. The double ionization of oxygen (two electrons ejected from the oxygen atom) requires temperatures around 100,000 degrees Kelvin, which astounded astronomers of that time, as this was almost twenty times greater than the surface temperature of the sun. Today, we know that those temperatures are easily reached by the hot central stars of planetary nebulae. These stars can range from 30,000 to 150,000 degrees Kelvin, making them the hottest stars in the universe.

M20
TRIFID NEBULA

Also cataloged as NGC 6514. Constellation: Sagittarius. Distance: 5,500 to 9,000 light years.

Right Ascension: 18 hours : 02.3 minutes
Declination: -23 degrees : 02 minutes

A celebrated gem of the summer sky, the Trifid Nebula allows us a view into the exciting science of star birth. The young HII region is about 30 light years across and illuminated by an O-type supergiant star at the center of its trilobed emission cloud. The ionizing star has about thirty times the mass of our sun and forms one component of a triple star system. In all, seven stars are packed within a half light year at the center of the Trifid Nebula. A large blue reflection cloud forms the nebula's northern border and is illuminated separately by an F-type supergiant star. Recent X-ray and infrared observations have discovered an amazing array of very early stars and protostars in the Trifid Nebula, giving us a rare glimpse of the earliest stages of star birth.

M8

LAGOON NEBULA

Also cataloged as NGC 6532 and popularly known as the Hourglass Nebula.
Constellation: Sagittarius. Distance: 5,800 light years.

Right Ascension: 18 hours : 03.8 minutes
Declination: -24 degrees : 23 minutes

A dark lane of dust divides M8 like a black lagoon, giving the HII region its popular name. Similar to other bright HII regions, the Lagoon Nebula exists as a thin blister of excited gas on the surface of a giant molecular cloud. Several massive O-type  giants in the bright young star cluster NGC 6530 illuminate the east side of the lagoon. The brightest part of the nebula, known as the "hourglass" because of it distinctive shape, is excited by two massive O-type supergiants that lie to the west of the lagoon. Remarkably, at least sixty B-type giants are embedded in the nebula, making the Lagoon Nebula three to four times richer in massive stars than the Orion Nebula.

N
E

NGC 6559

Constellation: Sagittarius. Distance: 5,800 light years.

Right Ascension: 18 hours : 10.0 minutes
Declination: -24 degrees : 06 minutes

The NGC 6559 complex is a colorful tapestry of diverse types of nebulosity. The glowing red cloud NGC 6559 formed from the same molecular cloud that gave rise to its neighbor the Lagoon Nebula. The region is awash in young stars, many of which are obscured by the region's ubiquitous dust. Within the nebula complex are several bright blue reflection clouds, glowing by way of starlight reflected from innumerable microscopic dust particles enveloping the brighter stars.

M16

EAGLE NEBULA

Constellation: Serpens. Distance: 7,000 light years.

Right Ascension: 18 hours : 18.8 minutes
Declination: -13 degrees : 47 minutes

Similar to earthly sandstone buttes, the giant pillars of the Eagle Nebula have survived the erosion of their surrounding landscape. The flood of ultraviolet radiation from the young star cluster NGC 6611 (upper right) has boiled away the less dense gas, leaving the denser material of the famous column structures intact. The star cluster illuminates the gas pillars, known as Evaporating Gaseous Globules, or EGGs. Protostars have been forming for thousands of years in the EGGs; however, their evolution is likely halted as the gaseous cocoons that fed their growth are lifted away. Protostars are not often observed directly, being cloaked by opaque gas and dust until they emerge as main sequence stars. The Eagle Nebula presents a rare opportunity to observe these infant stars as they emerge prematurely from the evaporating pillars. In fact, the infant stars of the Eagle Nebula may be the earliest stages of protostars ever observed.

M17
SWAN NEBULA

Also popularly known as the Omega Nebula, the Horseshoe Nebula, or the Lobster Nebula.
Constellation: Sagittarius. Distance: 5,000 light years.

Right Ascension: 18 hours : 20.8 minutes
Declination: -16 degrees : 11 minutes

The Swan Nebula is one of the largest HII region–molecular cloud complexes in the inner part of our galaxy and one of the closest to our sun. It is located in the Sagittarius arm. The Swan Nebula is the prototypical example of triggered star formation, where an HII region expands into an adjacent molecular cloud, triggering fragmentation and core collapse in the cloud and producing a cascade of new star formation. The massive star cluster NGC 6618, obscured by dust and gas, illuminates the Swan Nebula. The cluster's rich core contains up to one hundred of the most massive hot O- and B-type stars.

M22

Also cataloged as NGC 6656. Constellation: Sagittarius. Distance: 10,400 light years.

Right Ascension: 18 hours : 36.4 minutes
Declination: -23 degrees : 54 minutes

M22 ranks third in brightness among the 150 known Milky Way globulars. Only the bright southern globulars, Omega Centauri and 47 Tucanae, visually outshine M22. One of only four globulars known to harbor a planetary nebula, M22 stretches some 200 light years across. It is also one of the nearest globulars to our sun. M22 is considered an old globular cluster having its beginning some 12 billion years ago, not long after the formation of the Milky Way.

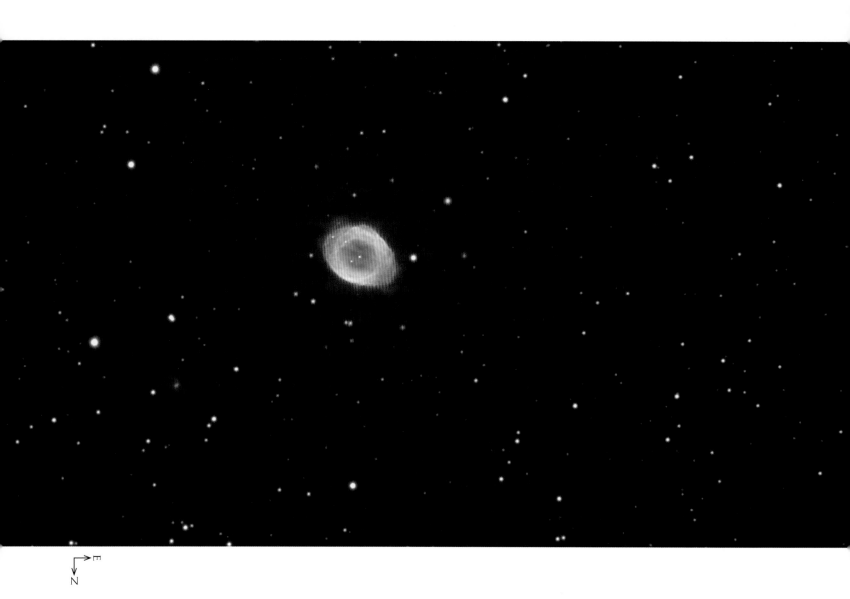

M57

RING NEBULA

Also cataloged as NGC 6720. Constellation: Lyra. Distance: 1,630 light years.

Right Ascension: 18 hours : 53.6 minutes
Declination: +33 degrees : 02 minutes

One of the best examples of a planetary nebula, the Ring Nebula represents the gaseous remains of a sunlike star. The intense radiation from the stellar remnant ionizes the star's previously ejected gases. The inner shell glows green from ionized oxygen and nitrogen, while hydrogen in the outer shell glows red. The stellar object in the center is a planet-sized white dwarf. Now over 100,000 degrees Kelvin, the white dwarf produces heat not by nuclear fusion but by its incredible density. The planetary-nebula stage lasts only ten thousand to thirty thousand years, an astronomical instant in the overall life of a star. Astronomers estimate the age of the Ring Nebula at 6,000 to 8,000 years old.

M54

NUCLEUS OF THE SAGITTARIUS DWARF ELLIPTICAL GALAXY

Constellation: Sagittarius. Distance: 85,000 light years.

Right Ascension: 18 hours : 55.1 minutes
Declination: -30 degrees : 29 minutes

The globular cluster M54 was discovered in 1778, but in 1994, velocity measurements of its stars indicated that it was outside our Milky Way galaxy—making it the first extragalactic globular cluster ever detected. The cluster is now thought to be the surviving nucleus of the Sagittarius Dwarf Elliptical Galaxy (called SagDEG), which cannot be imaged because it is obscured behind the central bulge of the Milky Way. The globular cluster coincides with one of two bright knots in the center of the dwarf galaxy and is receding at the same velocity.

The main body of SagDEG extends across some 20 degrees of sky, making it the largest apparent structure in the sky after the Milky Way itself. Astronomers believe it is a satellite galaxy currently being cannibalized by our galaxy. Its diameter measures about 28,000 light years, although its mass is only a thousandth of the Milky Way. The dwarf galaxy is so large and extended that it represents a barely perceptible increased stellar concentration from the sky foreground.

Z← E

NGC 6744

Constellation: Pavo. Distance: 36 million light years.

Right Ascension: 19 hours : 09.8 minutes
Declination: -63 degrees : 51 minutes

The spectacular barred galaxy NGC 6744 in the southern sky bears graceful spiral arms and is similar in many respects (size, central bar, spiral arm morphology, chemical abundances) to the Milky Way. One of the largest galaxies beyond the Local Group, NGC 6744 belongs to the Pavo-Indus galaxy cloud and is relatively isolated with no large companions.

NGC 6823

Constellation: Vulpecula. Distance: 8,150 light years.

Right Ascension: 19 hours : 43.1 minutes
Declination: +23 degrees : 18 minutes

The open cluster NGC 6823 represents the bright central core cluster of the Vulpecula OB1 stellar association, a network of young stars in the Orion arm of our galaxy. The cluster illuminates the area of mixed emission and reflection clouds known as NGC 6820. Dispersed among the surrounding nebulosity is a host of dark clouds, gas pillars, and several Bok globules. The stars of NGC 6823 formed between two million and five million years ago.

NGC 6822

BARNARD'S GALAXY

Constellation: Sagittarius. Distance: 1.6 million light years.

Right Ascension: 19 hours : 44.9 minutes
Declination: -14 degrees: 48 minutes

Discovered by the astronomer and astrophotographer Edward Barnard in 1884, Barnard's Galaxy is an irregular dwarf galaxy of the Magellanic type. It lies fourth-nearest to the Milky Way after the Sagittarius Dwarf Elliptical Galaxy and the Magellanic Clouds. In 1925 in a classic paper, Edwin Hubble reported that Barnard's Galaxy contained several bright objects, later found to represent a grouping of bright star clusters and HII regions. Prominent HII regions and scattered clusters of young blue stars testify to the galaxy's current high rate of star formation.

N
E

M27

DUMBBELL NEBULA

Also cataloged as NGC 6853. Constellation: Vulpecula. Distance: 1,200 light years.

Right Ascension: 19 hours: 59.6 minutes
Declination: +22 degrees : 43 minutes

M27 holds the distinction of being the first planetary nebula ever discovered, in 1764. Messier's description of it as an "oval nebula without stars" was followed by John Herschel's comparison to a dumbbell, which eventually became its popular name. The outer shell of the Dumbbell Nebula represents the ionization of gases released many thousands of years earlier. The nebula appears to be expanding at a rate of 6.8 arcseconds per century, which suggests an age of three thousand to four thousand years. High-energy radiation from the central white dwarf is absorbed by the gases of the nebula and re-emitted predominantly in green light due to ionized oxygen.

N
E

NGC 6888

CRESCENT NEBULA

Constellation: Cygnus. Distance: 4,700 light years.

Right Ascension: 20 hours : 12.0 minutes
Declination: +38 degrees : 21 minutes

A powerful Wolf-Rayet, visible as a blue star near the center of the shell-like nebula, provides the sole energy source of the Crescent Nebula. The star began its life some 4.5 million years ago as an extremely luminous and hot O-type supergiant. The physical structure of the Crescent Nebula was formed from material lost by the star during its red giant phase and later swept up by the furious wind of the Wolf-Rayet phase. Subsequently, the shell thinned and fragmented and became ionized by the ultraviolet flux of the central star. Presently, the nebula consists of a network of clumps and filaments that shine from the ionizing field of the central star.

IC 1318

BUTTERFLY NEBULA

Constellation: Cygnus. Distance: 5,000 light years.

Right Ascension: 20 hours : 22.2 minutes
Declination: +40 degrees : 15 minutes

The giant HII region IC 1318 spans some 100 light years. The symmetry of the bright complex explains why it is popularly referred to as the Butterfly Nebula. Although projected in the center of the nebulosity, the blue star Sadr, or Gamma Cygni, actually lies in the foreground at a distance of only 750 light years (wide-angle view at right). It is not related to the nebula, which is located much farther away at about 5,000 light years. The entire HII region is illuminated by a heavily obscured but powerful O-type star embedded deep within the clouds and visible only at infrared wavelengths. The thick intervening dust of the Milky Way considerably obscures the entire region.

N←
↓
E

NGC 6914

Constellation: Cygnus. Distance: 5,000 light years.

Right Ascension: 20 hours : 24.7 minutes
Declination: +42 degrees : 29 minutes

A complex of emission nebulae and icy blue reflection clouds, NGC 6914 is the tip of a celestial iceberg. Its stars belong to the vast Cygnus OB2 association, arguably the most massive and extensive stellar association in the Milky Way. Its total mass is estimated to be several hundred thousand solar masses but it is mostly invisible to telescope view because of the great dust clouds of the Milky Way. The southern and northern reflection clouds in the photograph are known as NGC 6914A and NGC 6914B, respectively.

E
Z

NGC 6946

Constellation: Cepheus. Distance: 19 million light years.

Right Ascension: 20 hours : 34.8 minutes
Declination: +60 degrees : 09 minutes

High levels of star formation occur throughout the disk of NGC 6946, one of the nearest giant spiral galaxies beyond the Local Group. It has a peculiar multiple-arm spiral structure that coalesces into four dominant spiral arms. NGC 6946 has hosted a record eight supernovae within the last century, attesting to its prodigious star-forming history. Because the galaxy is located at a low galactic latitude, its light is significantly reddened by foreground dust in the Milky Way.

NGC 7000 and IC 5070

NORTH AMERICAN AND PELICAN NEBULAE

Constellation: Cygnus. Distance: 1,800 light years.

Right Ascension: 20 hours : 50.8 minutes
Declination: +44 degrees : 21 minutes

The North American and Pelican Nebulae count among the greatest nebulae of the summer sky. The visible clouds appear as two distinct objects separated by a thick dust lane. Surveys at radio wavelengths have added to our understanding of the complex's underlying gaseous structure. The glowing clouds and dust lane belong to a more expansive but optically invisible molecular cloud. The cloud's dust component hides the massive O-type star that illuminates the nebula and causes it to fluoresce.

IC 5067 (below) is a fascinating region representing the "neck" of the Pelican Nebula. Massive stars hidden behind the region's thick dust release a prodigious flood of intense ultraviolet radiation that wreaks havoc on the local environment. The radiation ionizes parts of the molecular cloud while eroding and evaporating other areas. Higher density matter resists ionization and survives as long globules of dust and gas. Jets of hot gas, ejected from the heads of some of the prominent pillars, indicate newly forming stars within the globules.

151

Z ←
E ↓

NGC 6960, NGC 6992, and NGC 6995

CYGNUS LOOP

Also popularly known as the Veil Nebula or the Bridal Veil. Constellation: Cygnus. Distance: 1,500 light years.

Right Ascension: 20 hours : 56.4 minutes
Declination: +31 degrees : 43 minutes

One day long ago, prior to the dawn of recorded history, a brilliant light flashed in the night sky, unrivaled by anything seen before. The new "star" undoubtedly captured the imagination of prehistoric observers who, as the light faded from sight over several weeks, struggled to explain its origin and interpret its meaning. We now know the flash represented a rare supernova occurring in our own galaxy some ten thousand years ago. Although the blast annihilated the star, it left an immense glowing nebulous arc in its wake, which we now call the Cygnus Loop (right) or the Veil Nebula.

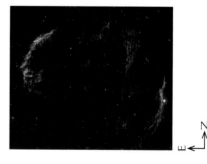

N ↑
E ←

The Cygnus Loop spans some 80 light years and 3 degrees of summer sky in the constellation Cygnus. The shock wave of the supernova created the delicate tendrils of glowing gas. The material blasted from the dying star collides with stationary ambient gases of the interstellar medium at speeds up to 1.4 million kilometers per hour, energizing the gas molecules. The gases release the newly acquired energy in different wavelengths, including the brilliant colors of the visual spectrum. In some regions, the gases heat to millions of degrees, causing the release of high-energy X-rays.

The western arc of the Cygnus Loop is cataloged as NGC 6960 (top). NGC 6992 and NGC 6995 make up the eastern front of the expanding arc. The bright star centered within NGC 6960 is actually an unrelated foreground star. The supernova remnant will dissipate over thousands of years, returning its heavier elements, such as gold, calcium, and iron, to the interstellar medium.

NGC 7023

Iris Nebula

Constellation: Cepheus. Distance: 1,400 light years.

Right Ascension: 21 hours : 00.5 minutes
Declination: +68 degrees : 10 minutes

A bright star shines through the Iris Nebula like a beacon through a celestial fog. The illuminating star of the reflection nebula is centrally embedded in a region cloaked by thick obscuring dust clouds. The blue starlight reflects from the surface of innumerable minute dust particles. The nebula also emits radiation from its microscopic dust particles, mostly in the infrared. We see the optical counterpart of this emission in the low-level red light of the dark dust clouds surrounding the bright nebula on its south and west side. The Iris Nebula is located at the northern end of a vast and optically invisible molecular cloud.

M39

Also cataloged as NGC 7092. Constellation: Cygnus. Distance: 900 light years.

Right Ascension: 21 hours : 32.2 minutes
Declination: +48 degrees : 26 minutes

M39 is a very sparse cluster of thirty or so stars spread over an area of about 7 light years. Its members are all still on the main sequence, but several of the brighter stars will soon become red giants. The stars of M39 are about 250 million years old, which makes it a middle-aged cluster. M39 is framed against the star clouds and dust lanes of the Cygnus Milky Way.

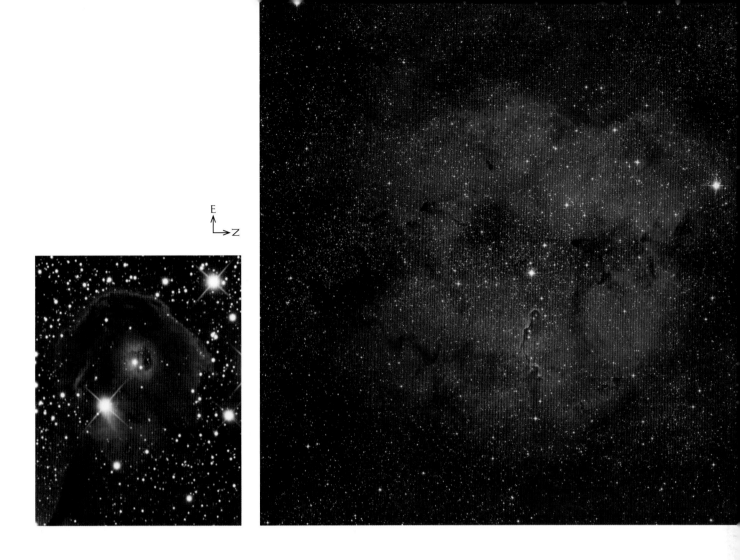

E
Z

IC 1396

Also cataloged as S131. Constellation: Cepheus. Distance: 2,400 light years.

Right Ascension: 21 hours : 39.1 minutes
Declination: +57 degrees : 30 minutes

The large HII region IC 1396 in the constellation Cepheus spans some 3 degrees of winter sky. It is illuminated by a single massive O-type supergiant blue star, located at the center of the donut-shaped emission cloud. Just to the north of IC 1396 shines the bright yellow supergiant star Mu Cephei. It has the distinction of being one of the most luminous stars in our galaxy, emitting 350,000 times the power of our sun.

Several cometlike structures, known as bright rimmed globules, form a loose and slowly expanding ring within IC 1396. Although several of the cometary globules are optically conspicuous, the most prominent and well-studied is IC 1396A (left), popularly known as the Elephant Trunk Nebula. Bright rimmed globules and their more evolved cousins, cometary globules, result from the fascinating dynamic interplay of cold molecular clouds and hot ionizing stars. Typically, the head of the globule faces a hot O-type star, which boils away lower-density gas from the head, leaving the denser material of the globule. The globules often become fertile areas of low-mass star formation. Within the center of the Elephant Trunk Nebula are several newborn glowing stars, which have hollowed out a cavity and energized a small glowing HII cloud.

NGC 7129

Constellation: Cepheus. Distance: 3,300 light years.

Right Ascension: 21 hours : 41.3 minutes
Declination: +66 degrees : 06 minutes

NGC 7129 is a young, compact star-forming region that displays an unusually striking tapestry of colorful nebulosity and bright stars contrasted against the dark clouds of the Milky Way. The astronomical counterpart to those colors and textures is the rich interplay that occurs between young stars and the surrounding interstellar medium. NGC 7129 contains several bright reflection nebulae, including the blue reflection cloud NGC 7133 and the unusual yellow reflection cloud LBN 497. Conspicuous in the field are several bright Herbig-Haro objects (glowing red patches), the signatures of young stellar objects soon to emerge into the main sequence and become full-fledged stars.

IC 5146

COCOON NEBULA

Constellation: Cygnus. Distance: 3,900 light years.

Right Ascension: 21 hours: 53.4 minutes
Declination: +47 degrees : 16 minutes

The beautiful emission and reflection cloud known as the Cocoon Nebula surrounds its massive ionizing central star. The colorful nebula is located at the eastern end of a series of dark clouds. The cluster of stars at the center of the Cocoon Nebula comprise mostly low-mass stars like our sun, only much younger at about one million years old—very young for a star! The cluster is so young that many of its members are still pre-main-sequence stars.

INDEX

ABOUT THE AUTHOR/PHOTOGRAPHER

Robert Gendler is a physician by profession. His love for space was born in the theater of the Hayden Planetarium where he made frequent school trips as a youngster growing up in New York City. Pursuing his childhood dream, he took up astrophotography later in his adult life and before long, it blossomed into a consuming and passionate avocation and means of self-expression. Self-taught and artistically innovative, Dr. Gendler went on to become a world-renowned astrophotographer and an acknowledged pioneer in CCD astrophotography. His original methods and inventive imaging philosophy have advanced the world of CCD astroimaging. His images have been published worldwide in many venues including the web, books, magazines, calendars, movies, and documentaries.

Dr. Gendler's work has been published on the acclaimed NASA website, "Astronomy Picture of the Day," more than any other amateur astrophotographer in the world. His image of the Andromeda Galaxy was selected as one of the greatest astronomical images of the last thirty years by *Astronomy* magazine in September 2003. His work routinely appears in popular astronomy periodicals such as *Sky & Telescope* and *Astronomy*, as well as many international astronomy magazines and books throughout the world. Dr. Gendler lives in Avon, Connecticut.